# BEARS I HAVE MET--AND OTHERS

by

## ALLEN KELLY

\

# CONTENTS

## PREFACE

These bear stories were accumulated and written during a quarter of a century of intermittent wanderings and hunting on the Pacific Slope, and are here printed in a book because they may serve to entertain and amuse. Most of them are true, and the others--well, every hunter and fisherman has a certain weakness, which is harmless, readily detected and sympathetically tolerated by others of the guild. The reader will not be deceived by the whimsical romances of the bear-slayers, and he may rest assured that these tales illustrate many traits of the bear and at least one trait of the men who hunt him.

One of the most amiable and well-behaved denizens of the forest, Bruin has ever been an outlaw and a fugitive with a price on his pelt and no rights which any man is bound to respect.

Like most outlawed men, he has been supplied with a reputation much worse than he deserves as an excuse for his persecution and a justification to his murderers. His character has been traduced in tales of the fireside and his disposition has been maligned ever since the female of his species came out of the woods to rebuke irreverence to smooth-pated age. Every man's hand has been against him, but seldom has his paw been raised against man except in self-defense.

A vegetarian by choice and usually by necessity, Bruin is accused of anthropophagy, and every child is taught that the depths of the woodland are infested by ravening bears with a morbid taste for tender youth. Poor, harried, timid Ursus, nosing among the fallen leaves for acorns and beechnuts, and ready to flee like a startled hare at the sound of a foot-fall, is represented in story and picture as raging through the forest with slavering jaws seeking whom he may devour. Yet the man does not live who can say truthfully that he ever was eaten by a bear.

Possibly there have been bears of abnormal or vitiated tastes who have indulged in human flesh, just as there are men who eat decayed cheese and "high" game, but the gustatory sins of such perverts may not be visited justly on the species. There are few animals so depraved in taste as to dine off man except under stress of famine, and Bruin is not one of the few. He is no epicure, but he draws the line at the lord of creation flavored with tobacco.

I have a suspicion that some of the tales told around campfires and here set down might be told differently if the bears could talk. It is a pity they can't talk, for they are very human in other ways and have a sense of humor that would make their versions of some "true bear stories" vastly amusing. What delightful reading, for example, would be the impressions made by a poet of the Sierra upon the bears he has met! Perhaps no bear ever met a poet of the Sierra, but mere unacquaintance with the subject should be no more of a disadvantage to a bear than to a man of letters.

## CHAPTER I: THE CALIFORNIA GRIZZLY.

The California Grizzly made his reputation as a man-killer in the days of the muzzle-loading rifle, when failure to stop him with one shot deprived the hunter of all advantage in respect of weapons and reversed their positions instantly, the bear becoming the hunter and the man the game. In early days, also the Grizzly had no fear of man and took no pains to keep out of his way, and bears were so numerous that chance meetings at close quarters were frequent.

But with all of his ferocity when attacked and his formidable strength, the Grizzly's resentment was often transitory, and many men owe their lives to his singular lack of persistency in wreaking his wrath upon a fallen foe. Generalizations on the conduct of animals, other than in the matter of habits of life governed by what we call instinct, are likely to be misleading, and when applied to animals of high intelligence and well-developed individuality, are utterly valueless. I have found the Grizzly more intelligent than other American bears and his individual characteristics more marked and varied, and therefore am disinclined to formulate or accept any rules of conduct for him under given circumstances. No man can say what a Grizzly will or will not do, when molested or encountered, any more than he can lay down a general rule for dogs or men. One bear may display extreme timidity and run away bawling when wounded, and another may be aggressive enough to begin hostilities at sight and fight to the death. It can be said safely, however, that the Grizzly is a far more dangerous animal than the Black Bear and much more likely to accept a challenge than to run away.

Want of persistent vindictiveness may not be a general trait of the species, but it has been shown in so many cases that it is at least a quite common characteristic. Possibly it is a trait of all bears and the basis of the almost universal belief that a bear will not molest a dead man, and that by "playing 'possum" a person attacked by a bear may evade further injury. That belief or theory has been held from the earliest times, and it is by no means certain that it is a mere idle tale or bit of nursery lore. Aesop uses it in one of his fables. Two men are assailed by a bear, and one climbs a tree while the other throws himself upon the ground and feigns death. The bear sniffs at the man on the ground, who holds his breath, concludes that the man is dead, and goes away. The man who climbed the tree rejoins his companion, and having seen the bear sniffing at his head, asks him facetiously what the bear said to him. The man who played 'possum replies that the bear told him to beware of keeping company with those who in time of danger leave their friends in the lurch.

This I do know, that bears often invade camps in search of food and refrain from molesting men asleep or pretending to be asleep. Upon one occasion a Grizzly of very bad reputation and much feared by residents in his district, came into my camp on a pitch dark night, and as it would have been futile to attempt to draw a bead on him and a fight would have endangered two members of the party who were incapable of defending themselves, I cautioned everyone to feign sleep and not to show signs of life if the bear sniffed in their faces. The injunction was obeyed, the bear satisfied his curiosity, helped himself to food and went away without molesting anybody.

And that is not an isolated instance. One night a Grizzly invaded a bivouac, undeterred by the still blazing fire, and tried to reach a haunch of venison hung upon a limb directly over one of the party. The man--Saml Snedden, the first settler in Lockwood Valley, Cal.-- awoke and saw the great beast towering over him and stretching up in a vain effort to reach the venison, and he greatly feared that in coming down to all fours again the bear might forget his presence and step upon him. Snedden tried furtively to draw his rifle out from the blankets in which he had enveloped it, but found that he could not get the weapon, without attracting the bear's attention and probably provoking immediate attack. So he abandoned the attempt, kept perfectly still and watched the bear with half-closed eyes. The

Grizzly realized that the meat was beyond his reach, and with a sighing grunt came down to all fours, stepping upon and crushing flat a tin cup filled with water within a foot of the man's head. The bear inquisitively turned the crushed cup over, smelt of it, sniffed at Snedden's ear and slouched slowly away into the darkness as noiselessly as a phantom, and only one man in the camp knew he had been there except by the sign of his footprints and the flattened cup.

Many hunters have told me of similar experiences, and never have I heard of one instance of unprovoked attack upon a sleeping person by a bear, or for that matter by any other of the large carnivorae of this country. Only one authentic instance of a bear feeding on human flesh have I known, and that was under unusual circumstances.

Two things will be noted by the reader of these accounts of California bear fights: First, that the Grizzly's point of attack is usually the face or head, and second, that, except in the case of she-bears protecting or avenging their cubs, the Grizzly ceased his attack when satisfied that his enemy was no longer capable of continuing the fight, and showed no disposition to wantonly mangle an apparently dead man. Since the forty she-bears came out of the wilderness and ate up a drove of small boys for guying a holy man, who was unduly sensitive about his personal dignity, the female of the ursine species, however, has been notorious for ill-temper and vindictive pertinacity, and she maintains that reputation to this day.

In the summer of 1850, G. W. Applegate and his brother John were mining at Horse Shoe Bar on the American River. The nearest base of supplies at that time was Georgetown, eighteen miles distant by trail. One evening in early summer, having run short of provisions, George and his brother started to walk to that camp to make purchases. Darkness soon overtook them and while descending into Canyon Creek they heard a bear snort at some distance behind. In a few moments they heard it again, louder than before, and John rather anxiously remarked that he thought the bear was following them. George thought not, but in a few seconds after crossing the stream and beginning the ascent upon the other side, both distinctly heard him come--splash, splash, splash--through the water directly upon their trail.

It was as dark as Erebus, and they were without weapons larger than pocket knives--a serious position with an angry Grizzly dogging their steps. Their first thought was to climb a tree, but knowing they were not far from the cabin of a man named Work, they took to their heels and did their best running to reach that haven of refuge ahead of their formidable follower. They reached the cabin, rushed in, slammed and fastened the door behind them, and with breathless intervals gasped out their tale. Work kept a bar for the sale of whiskey, and he and his son, a stout young man, with two or three miners, were sitting on rude seats around a whiskey barrel playing cards when the two frightened men rushed in.

The cabin was built by planting posts firmly in the ground at a distance of some three feet apart, and in the form of a parallelogram, then nailing shakes upon these posts and on the roof. The sides were held together by cross beams, connecting the tops of the opposite posts. There was one rude window, made by cutting a hole in the side of the wall about four feet from the ground and covering this with greased paper, glass being an unattainable luxury. Notwithstanding the belief that there was not a man in those days but wore a red shirt and a big revolver, there was not a firearm in the place.

In a few seconds the bear was heard angrily sniffing at the door, and an instant later his powerful paw came tearing through the frail shakes and he poked his head and neck through the opening and gravely surveyed the terrified party. Every man sprang upon the bar and thence to the cross beam with the alacrity given only by terror. After sniffing a moment and calmly gazing around the room and up at the frightened men, the bear quietly withdrew his head and retired.

After an interval of quiet, the men ventured down and were eagerly discussing the event, when the bear again made its presence known by rearing up and thrusting its head through the paper of the window. Upon this occasion some of the men stood their ground, and young Work, seizing an iron-pointed Jacob's staff, ran full tilt at the bear, and thrust it deeply into its chest. The bear again disappeared, taking the Jacob's staff, and appeared no more that night.

The following morning, search being made, the bear was found dead some yards from the cabin, with the staff thrust through the heart. It proved to be a female and was severely wounded in several places with rifle balls.

Subsequent inquiries elicited the fact that on the previous day a party of hunters from Georgetown had captured two cubs and wounded the mother, which had escaped. This was evidently the same bear in search of her cubs.

* * * * *

In the spring of the year, somewhere early in the fifties, a party of five left the mining camp of Coloma for the purpose of hunting deer for the market in the locality of Mosquito Canyon. On the morning of the second day in camp the party separated, each going his own way to hunt, and at night it was found that one of their members named Broadus failed to appear. The others started out in different directions to search for him the next morning, and after a day spent in fruitless searching, they returned to camp only to find that another of their number, named William Jabine, was this night missing.

After an anxious night, chiefly spent in discussing the probable fate of their missing companions, the remaining three started out on the trail of Jabine, he having told them the previous morning what part of the country he was going to travel. Slowly following his tracks left in the soft soil and broken down herbage, they found him about noon, terribly mangled and unconscious, but alive. The flesh on his face was torn and lacerated in a frightful manner, and he was otherwise injured in his chest and body.

Further search revealed, near by, the dead body of their other missing comrade, seated on a bowlder by the side of a small stream with his head on his folded arms, which were supported by a shelf of rock in front of him. His whole under jaw had been bitten off and torn away, and a large pool of clotted blood at his feet showed that he had slowly bled to death after having been attacked and wounded by a bear. The ground showed evidences of a fearful struggle, being torn up and liberally sprinkled with blood for yards around.

The men carried Jabine to the nearest mining camp, whence others went to bring in the body of Broadus.

Jabine finally recovered, but he was shockingly disfigured for life. He afterwards told how he came upon the tracks of Broadus, and on reaching the spot where Broadus had received his death wound, he was suddenly attacked by a huge she-bear that was followed by two small cubs. The bear had evidently been severely wounded by Broadus and was in a terrible rage. She seized Jabine before he could turn to flee, and falling with her whole weight upon his body and chest, began biting his face. He soon lost consciousness from the pressure upon his chest, and remembered no more.

The poor fellow became a misanthrope, owing to his terrible disfigurement, and was finally found drowned in the river near Coloma.

In 1850 a number of miners were camped upon the spot where the little town of Todd's Valley now stands. Among them were three brothers named Gaylord, who had just arrived from Illinois. These young men used to help out the proceeds of their claim by an occasional hunt, taking their venison down to the river when killed, where a carcass was readily disposed of for two ounces.

One evening when the sun was about an hour high, one of the brothers took his rifle and went out upon the hills and did not return that night. The following morning his two brothers set out in search and soon found him dead, bitten through the spine in the neck, evidently by a bear. His rifle was unloaded and the tracks showed where he had fled, pursued by the angry animal, been overtaken, and killed.

On the succeeding day a hunt was organized and some twenty men turned out to seek revenge. The bears, for there were two of them, were tracked into a deep rocky canyon running from Forest Hill to Big Bar. Large rocks were rolled down its sides, and the bears were routed out and both killed.

In 1851, three men armed with Kentucky rifles, which were not only muzzle-loaders, but of small calibre and less effective than the ordinary .32 calibre rifle of to-day, were hunting deer on the divide between Volcano and Shirttail Canyons in Placer county. In the heavy timber on the slope they encountered a large Grizzly coming up out of Volcano Canyon. The bear was a hundred yards distant when they saw him and evinced no desire for trouble, and two of the hunters were more than willing to give him the trail and let him go about his business in peace. The other, a man named Wright, who had killed small bears, but knew nothing about the Grizzly, insisted on attacking, and prepared to shoot. The others assured him that a bullet from a Kentucky rifle at that distance would only provoke the bear to rush them, and begged him not to fire. But Wright laughed at them and pulled trigger with a bead on the bear's side, where even a heavy ball would be wasted.

The Grizzly reared upon his haunches, bit at the place where the ball stung him, and after waving his paws in the air two or three times, came directly for Wright with a fierce growl. The party all took to their heels and separated, but the bear soon overtook Wright and with one blow of his paw struck the man, face downward, upon the snow and began biting him about the head, back and arms. The other hunters, seeing the desperate case of their companion, rushed up and fired at the bear at close range, fortunately killing him with a bullet in the base of the brain.

Wright, on being relieved of the weight of his antagonist, sat up in a dazed condition, with the blood pouring in streams down his face. He had received several severe bites in the back and arms, but the worst wound was on the head, where the bear had struck him with his claws. His scalp was almost torn from his head, and a large piece of skull some three inches in diameter was broken out and lifted from the brain as cleanly as if done by the surgeon's trephine.

Strange to say, Wright complained of but little pain, excepting from a bite in the arm, and soon recovered his senses. His comrades replaced the mangled scalp, and bleeding soon ceased. A fire was built to keep him warm and while one watched with the wounded man the other returned to the trail to intercept a pack train. On the arrival of the mules, Wright was helped upon one of their backs, and rode unaided to the Baker ranch.

A surgeon was sent for from Greenwood Valley, who, on his arrival, removed the loose piece of bone from the skull and dressed the wounds. The membranes of the brain were uninjured, and the man quickly recovered, but of course had a dangerous hole in his skull that incapacitated him for work. One Sunday, some weeks afterward, the miners held a meeting, subscribed several hundred dollars and sent Wright home to his friends in Boston.

* * * * *

Mike Brannan was a miner on the Piru River in Southern California. The river, or creek, runs through a rough mountain district, and Brannan's claim was in the wildest part of it. He and his partner met a Grizzly on the trail, and Brannan had no better judgment than to fire his revolver at the bear instead of getting out of the way. The Grizzly charged, smashed the partner's skull with a blow and tumbled Brannan over a bank.

Brannan was stunned by the fall, and when consciousness returned he saw the bear standing across his body, watching him intently for signs of life. He tried to keep perfectly still and hold his breath, but the suspense was too great a strain and involuntarily he moved the fingers of his right hand. The bear did not see the movement, and when Brannan realized that his fingers had just touched his revolver, he conceived the desperate idea that he could reach the weapon and use it quickly enough to blow a hole through the bear's head and save himself from the attack which he felt he could not avert much longer by shamming.

To grasp the revolver it was necessary to stretch his arm full length, and he tried to do that slowly and imperceptibly, but his anxiety overcame his prudence and he made a movement that the watchful Grizzly detected. Instantly the bear pinned the arm with one paw, placed the other upon Brannan's breast and with his teeth tore out the biceps muscle. Brannan had the good luck to faint at that moment, and when his senses again returned he was alone. The Grizzly had watched him until satisfied that there was no more harm in him, and then left him.

Brannan managed to get to his cabin and eventually recovered, only to be murdered some years later for the gold dust he had stored away.

NOTE.--For many of the facts in this chapter of adventures with grizzlies in Placer and El Dorado counties in 1850 and 1851, I am indebted to Dr. R. F. Rooney, of Auburn, Cal., who obtained the details at first hand from pioneers.--A. K.

## CHAPTER II: THE STORY OF MONARCH.

Early in 1889, the editor of a San Francisco newspaper sent me out to catch a Grizzly. He wanted to present to the city a good specimen of the big California bear, partly because he believed the species was almost extinct, and mainly because the exploit would be unique in journalism and attract attention to his paper. Efforts to obtain a Grizzly by purchase and "fake" a story of his capture had proved fruitless for the sufficient reason that no captive Grizzly of the true California type could be found, and the enterprising journal was constrained to resort to the prosaic expedient of laying a foundation of fact and veritable achievement for its self-advertising.

The assignment was given to me because I was the only man on the paper who was supposed to know anything about bears. Such knowledge as I had, and it was not very extensive, had been acquired on hunting trips, some successful and more otherwise, in the Sierra Nevada and Cascades. I had had no experience in trapping, but I accepted the assignment with entire confidence and great joy over the chance to get into the mountains for a long outing. The outing proved to be much longer than the editor expected, and trapping a bear quite a different matter from killing one.

From Santa Paula, I struck into the mountains of Ventura county with an outfit largely composed of information, advice and over-paid assistance. The first two months of the trip were consumed in developing the inaccuracy of most of the information and the utter worthlessness of all the advice and costly assistance, and in acquiring some rudimentary knowledge of the habits of bears and the art of trapping them. Traps were built, under advice, where there was not one chance in a thousand of catching anything, and bogus bear-tracks, made with a neatly-executed model by an ingenious guide, who preferred loafing about camp to moving it, kept the expedition from seeking more promising country.

The editor became tired of waiting for his big sensation and ordered me home. I respectfully but firmly refused to go home bearless, and the editor fired me by wire. I fired the ingenious but sedentary assistant, discarded all the advice that had been unloaded upon me by the able bear-liars of Ventura, reduced my impedimenta to what one lone, lorn burro could pack, broke camp and struck for a better Grizzly pasture, determined to play the string out alone and in my own way. The place I selected for further operations was the regular beat of old Pinto, a Grizzly that had been killing cattle on Gen. Beale's range in the mountains west of Tehachepi and above Antelope Valley.

Old Pinto was no myth, and he didn't make tracks with a whittled pine foot. His lair was a dense manzanita thicket upon the slope of a limestone ridge about a mile from the spring by which I camped, and he roamed all over the neighborhood. In soft ground he made a track fourteen inches long and nine inches wide, but although at the time I took that for the size of his foot, I am now inclined to think that it was the combined track of front and hind foot, the hind foot "over-tracking" a few inches, obliterating the claw marks of the front foot and increasing the size of the imprint both in length and width. Nevertheless he was a very large bear, and he loomed up formidably in the dusk of an evening when I saw him feasting, forty yards away, upon a big steer he had killed.

Pinto had the reputation of being not only dangerous but malevolent, and there were oft told tales of domiciliary visits paid by him at the cabins of settlers, and of aggressive advances upon mounted vaqueros, who were saved by the speed of their horses. Doubtless the bear was audacious in foraging and indifferent to the presence of man, but he was not malevolent. Indeed, I have yet to hear on any credible authority of a malevolent bear, or, for that matter, any other wild animal in North America whose disposition and habit is to seek trouble with man and go out of its way with the deliberate purpose of attacking him. For many weeks I camped by that spring, much of the time alone, and without even a dog, with only a blanket for covering and the heavens for a roof, and my sleep never was disturbed by anything larger than a wood rat. My camp was on one of Pinto's beaten trails, but he abandoned it and passed fifty yards to one side or the other whenever his business took him down that way, and he never meddled with me or mine. One night, as his tracks showed, he came to within twenty feet of my bivouac, sniffed around inquiringly and passed on.

I built two stout traps for Pinto's benefit, and day after day I dragged bait around and through the manzanita thickets on the ridge and over all his trails, and sometimes I found tracks so fresh that I was satisfied he had heard me coming and had turned aside. There were cougar and lynx tracks all over the mountains, but I seldom saw the animals and then only got fleeting glimpses of them as they fled out of my way.

Many of my prejudices and all my story-book notions about the behavior of the carnivorae were discredited by experience, and I was forced to recognize the plain truth that the only mischievous animal, the only creature meditating and planning evil on that mountain--

excepting of course the evil incident to the procurement of food--was a man with a gun. I was the only really dangerous and unnecessarily destructive animal in the woods, and all the rest were afraid of me.

After a time, because I had no intention of killing Pinto if I should meet him, I quit carrying a rifle, except when I wanted venison, and tramped all over the mountain in daylight or in darkness without giving much thought to possible encounters. True, I carried a revolver, but that was force of habit mainly, and a six-shooter is company of a sort to a man in the wilderness even if he does not expect to need it. When one has "packed a gun" for years, he feels uncomfortable without it; not because he thinks he has any use for it, but because it has become a part of his attire and its absence unconsciously frets him and sets him wondering vaguely if he has lost his suspenders or forgotten to put on a tie.

That the big Grizzly was not quite so audacious and adventurous as he was reputed to be was demonstrated by his suspicious avoidance of the traps while they were new to him, and it became evident that he could not be inveigled into them even by meat and honey until they should become familiar objects to him and he should get accustomed to my scent upon his trails. That I would have caught old Pinto in time there is no doubt, for eventually he was caught in each of the traps, although he escaped through the carelessness of the man who baited and set them.

The traps were tight pens, built of large oak logs notched and pinned, roofed and floored with heavy logs and fitted with falling doors of four-inch plank. They were stout enough, and when I saw them ten years later they were sound and fit to hold anything that wears fur, although old Pinto had clawed all the bark off the logs and left deep furrows in them.

As a matter of course, all the hunters and mountain men for fifty miles around knew that I was trying to catch a Grizzly, and some of them built traps on their own hook, hoping to catch a bear and make a few dollars. I had encouraged them by promising to pay well for his trouble anybody who should get a bear in his own trap, or find one in any of the numerous traps I had built and send me word.

Late in October, I heard that a bear had got into a trap on Gleason Mountain, and leaving Pinto to his own devices, I went over to look at the captive. The Mexican acting as jailor did not know me, and I discovered that Allen Kelly was supposed to be the agent of a millionaire and an "easy mark," who would pay a fabulous sum for a bear. The Mexican assured me that he was about to get wealth beyond the dreams of avarice for that bear from a San Francisco man, meaning said Kelly, whereupon I congratulated him, disparaged the bear and turned to go. The Mexican followed me down the trail and began complaining that the alleged purchaser of the bear was dilatory in closing the deal with cash. He, Mateo, was aggrieved by this unbusinesslike behavior, and it would be no more than proper for him to resent it and teach the man a lesson in commercial manners by selling the bear to somebody else, even to me, for instance. Mateo's haste to get that bear off his hands was evident, but the reason for it was not apparent. Later I understood.

Monarch had the bad luck to get into a trap built by a little syndicate of which Mateo was a member. Mateo watched the trap, while the others supplied beef for bait. They were to divide the large sum which they expected to get from me in case they caught a bear before I did, and very likely my fired assistant had a contingent interest in the enterprise. Mateo was the only member of the syndicate on deck when I arrived, and deeming a bird in his hand worth a whole flock in the syndicate bush, he made the best bargain he could and left the others to whistle for dividends. Ten years afterward I met the cattleman who furnished the capital and the beef, and from his strenuous remarks about his Mexican partner I inferred that the syndicate had been deeply disappointed. I also learned for the first time why Mateo was so anxious for me to take the bear off his hands when the evident original purpose was to held me up for a good round sum. The hold-up would have failed, however, because I had spent more than $1,200 and lost five months' time, was nearly broke, did not represent anybody but myself at that stage of my bear-catching career, and for all I knew the editor might have changed his mind about wanting a Grizzly at any price.

Finally I consented to take the bear and struck a bargain, and not until money had passed and a receipt was to be signed did Mateo know with whom he was dealing. He paid me the dubious compliment of muttering that I was "un coyote," and as that animal is the B'rer Rabbit of Mexican folk lore, I inferred that the excellent Mateo intended to express admiration for the only evidence of business capacity to be found in my entire career. That dicker for a bear stands out as the sole trade I ever made in which I was not unmistakably and comprehensively "stuck." Mateo was more than repaid for his trouble, however. He helped me build a box, and get the bear into it, and I took Monarch to San Francisco and sold him to the editor of the enterprising paper, who eventually gave him to Golden Gate Park.

The newspaper account of the capture of Monarch was elaborated to suit the exigencies of enterprising journalism, picturesque features were introduced where the editorial judgment dictated, and mere facts, such as the name of the county in which the bear was caught, fell under the ban of a careless blue pencil and were distorted beyond recognition.

More than one-fourth of Joaquin Miller's "True Bear Stories"' consists of that newspaper yarn, copied verbatim and without amendment, revision or verification. The other three-fourths of the book, it is to be hoped, is at least equally true.

Considering all the frills of fiction that were put into the story to make it readable, the careless inaccuracies that were edited into it, and the fact that many persons knew of the preliminary attempts to buy any old bear and fake a capture, it is not strange that people who always know the "inside history" of everything that happens, wag their heads wisely and declare that Monarch was obtained from a bankrupt circus, or is an ex-dancer of the streets sold to the newspaper by a hard-up Italian.

But it is incredible that any one who knows a bear from a Berkshire hog could for an instant mistake Monarch for any variety of tamable bear or imagine that any man ever had the hardihood to give him dancing lessons.

When Monarch found himself caught in the syndicate trap on Gleason Mountain, he made furious efforts to escape. He bit and tore at the logs, hurled his great bulk against the sides and tried to enlarge every chink that admitted light. He required unremitting attention with a sharpened stake to prevent him from breaking out.

For a full week the Grizzly raged and refused to touch food that was thrown to him. Then he became exhausted and the task of securing him and removing him from the trap was begun. The first thing necessary was to make a chain fast to one of his fore-legs. That job was begun at eight o'clock in the morning and finished at six o'clock in the afternoon. Much time was wasted in trying to work with the chain between two of the side logs. Whenever the bear stepped into the loop as it lay upon the floor and the chain was drawn tight around his fore-leg just above the foot, he pulled it off easily with the other paw, letting the men who held the chain fall over backward. The feat was finally accomplished by letting the looped chain down between the roof logs, so that when the bear stepped into it and it was drawn sharply upward, it caught him well up toward the shoulder.

Having one leg well anchored, it was comparatively easy to introduce chains and ropes between the side logs and secure his other legs. He fought furiously during the whole operation, and chewed the chains until he splintered his canine teeth to the stubs and spattered the floor of the trap with bloody froth. It was painful to see the plucky brute hurting himself uselessly, but it could not be helped, as he would not give up while he could move limb or jaw.

The next operation was gagging the bear so that he could not bite. The door of the trap was raised and a billet of wood was held where he could seize it, which he promptly did. A cord made fast to the stick was quickly wound around his jaws, with turns around the stick on each side, and passed back of his ears and around his neck like a bridle. By that means his jaws were firmly bound to the stick in such a manner that he could not move them, while his mouth was left open for breathing.

While one man held the bear's head down by pressing with his whole weight upon the ends of the gag, another went into the trap and put a chain collar around the Grizzly's neck, securing it in place with a light chain attached to the collar at the back, passing down under his armpits and up to his throat, where it was again made fast. The collar passed through a ring attached by a swivel to the end of a heavy chain of Norwegian iron. A stout rope was fastened around the bear's loins also, and to this another strong chain was attached. This done, the gag was removed and the Grizzly was ready for his journey down the mountain.

In the morning he was hauled out of the trap and bound down on a rough skeleton sled made from a forked limb, very much like the contrivance called by lumbermen a "go-devil." Great difficulty was encountered in securing a team of horses that could be induced to haul the bear. The first two teams were so terrified that but little progress could be made, but the third team was tractable and the trip down the mountain to the nearest wagon road was finished in four days.

The bear was released from the "go-devil" and chained to trees every night; and so long as the camp fire burned brightly he would lie still and watch it attentively, but when the fire burned low he would get up and restlessly pace to and fro and tug at the chains, stopping now and then to seize in his arms the tree to which he was anchored and test its strength by shaking it. Every morning the same old fight had to be fought before he could be tied to his sled. He became very expert in dodging ropes and seizing them when the loops fell over his legs, and considerable strategic skill was required to lasso his paws and stretch him out. In the beginning of these contests the Grizzly uttered angry growls, but soon became silent and fought with dogged persistency, watching every movement of his foes with alert attention and wasting no energy in aimless struggles. He soon learned to keep his hind feet well under him and his body close to the ground, which left only his head and fore-legs to be defended from the ropes. So adroit and quick was the bear in the use of his paws that a dozen men could not get a rope on him while he remained in that posture of defence. But when two or three men grasped the chain that was around his body and suddenly threw him on his back, all four of his legs were in the air at once, the riatas flew from all directions and he was vanquished.

Monarch was pretty well worn out when the wagon road was reached, and doubtless enjoyed the few days of rest and quiet that were allowed him while a cage was being built for his further transportation. He made the remainder of the journey to San Francisco by wagon and railroad, confined in a box constructed of inch-and-a-half Oregon pine that had an iron grating at one end. The box was not strong enough to have held him for five minutes had he attacked it as he attacked the trap and as he subsequently demolished an iron-lined den, but I put my trust in the moral influence of the chain around his neck. The Grizzly accepted the situation resignedly and behaved admirably during the whole trip.

Monarch is the largest bear in captivity and a thoroughbred Californian Grizzly. No naturalist needs a second glance at him to classify him as Ursus Horribilis. He stands four feet high at the shoulder, measures three feet across the chest, 12 inches between the ears and 18 inches from ear to nose, and his weight is estimated by the best judges at from 1200 to 1600 pounds. He never has been weighed. In disposition he is independent and militant. He will fight anything from a crowbar to a powder magazine, and permit no man to handle him while he can move a muscle. And yet when he and I were acquainted--I have not seen him since he was taken to Golden Gate Park--he was not unreasonably quarrelsome, but preserved an attitude of armed neutrality. He would accept peace offerings from my hand, taking bits of sugar with care not to include my fingers, but would tolerate no petting. Within certain limits he would acknowledge an authority which had been made real to him by chains and imprisonment, and reluctantly suspend an intended blow and retreat to a corner when insistently commanded, yet the fires of rebellion never were extinguished and it would have been foolhardy to get within effective reach of his paw. To strangers he was irreconcilable and unapproachable.

Monarch passed three or four years in a steel cell before he was taken to the Park. He devoted a week or so to trying to get out and testing every bar and joint of his prison, and when he realized that his strength was over-matched, he broke down and sobbed. That was the critical point, and had he not been treated tactfully by Louis Ohnimus, doubtless the big Grizzly would have died of nervous collapse. A live fowl was put before him after he had refused food and disdained to notice efforts to attract his attention, and the old instinct to kill was aroused in him. His dulled eyes gleamed green, a swift clutching stroke of the paw secured the fowl. Monarch bolted the dainty morsel, feathers and all, and his interest in life was renewed with the revival of his savage propensity to slay.

From that moment he accepted the situation and made the best of it. He was provided with a bed of shavings, and he soon learned the routine of his keeper's work in removing the bed. Monarch would not permit the keeper to remove a single shaving from the cage if a fresh supply was not in sight. He would gather all the bedding in a pile, lie upon it and guard every shred jealously, striking and smashing any implement of wood or iron thrust into the cage to filch his treasure. But when a sackful of fresh shavings was placed where he could see it, Monarch voluntarily left his bed, went to another part of the cage and watched the removal of the pile without interfering.

In intelligence and quickness of comprehension, the Grizzly was superior to other animals in the zoological garden and compared not unfavorably with a bright dog. It could not be said of him, as of most other animals, that man's mastery of him was due to his failure to realize his own power. He knew his own strength and how to apply it, and only the superior strength of iron and steel kept him from doing all the damage of which he was capable.

The lions, for example, were safely kept in cages which they could have broken with a blow rightly placed. Monarch discovered the weak places of such a cage within a few hours and wrecked it with swift skill. When inveigled into a movable cage with a falling door, he turned the instant the door fell, seized the lower edge and tried to raise it. When placed in a barred enclosure in the park, he began digging under the stone foundation of the fence, necessitating the excavation of a deep trench and the emplacement therein of large boulders to prevent his escape. Then he tried the aerial route, climbed the twelve foot iron palings, bent the tops of inch and a half bars and was nearly over when detected and pushed back.

He remains captive only because it is physically impossible for him to escape, not because he is in the least unaware of his power or inept in using it. Apparently he has no illusions concerning man and no respect for him as a superior being. He has been beaten by superior cunning, but never conquered, and he gives no parole to refrain from renewing the contest when opportunity offers.

Mr. Ernest Thompson Seton saw Monarch and sketched him in 1901, and he said: "I consider him the finest Grizzly I have seen in captivity."

NOTE.--Without doubt the largest captive grizzly bear in the world, may be seen in the Golden Gate Park, San Francisco. As to his exact weight, there is much conjecture. That has not been determined, as the bear has never been placed on a scale. Good judges estimate it at not far from twelve hundred pounds. The bear's appearance justifies that conclusion. Monarch enjoys the enviable distinction of being the largest captive bear in the world.--N. Y. Tribune, March 8, 1903.

## CHAPTER III: CHRONICLES OF CLUBFOOT.

The most famous bear in the world was, is and will continue to be the gigantic Grizzly known variously on the Pacific Slope as "Old Brin," "Clubfoot," and "Reelfoot." He was first introduced to the public by a mining-camp editor named Townsend, who was nicknamed "Truthful James" in a spirit of playful irony. That was in the seventies. Old Erin was described as a bear of monstrous size, brindled coat, ferocious disposition and evil fame among the hunters of the Sierra. He had been caught in a steel trap and partly crippled by the loss of a toe and other mutilation of a front paw, and his clubfooted track was readily recognizable and served to identify him. Old Brin stood at least five feet high at the shoulder, weighed a ton or more and found no difficulty in carrying away a cow. He seemed to be impervious to bullets, and many hunters who took his trail never returned. A few who met him and had the luck to escape furnished the formidable details of his description and spread his fame, with the able assistance of Truthful James and other veracious historians of the California and Nevada press.

For several years the clubfooted Grizzly ranged the Sierra Nevada from Lassen county to Mono, invulnerable, invincible and mysterious, and every old hunter in the mountains had an awesome story to tell of the ferocity and uncanny craft of the beast and of his own miraculous escape from the jaws of the bear after shooting enough lead at him to start a smelter. Old Brin was a never-failing recourse of the country editor when the foreman was insistent for copy, and those who undertook to preserve the fame of his exploits in their files scrupulously respected the rights of his discoverer and never permitted any vain-glorious bear hunter to kill him. As one of the early guardians of this incomparable monster, I can bear witness that it was the unwritten law of the journalistic profession that no serious harm should come to the clubfoot bear and he should invariably triumph over his enemies. It was also understood that a specially interesting episode in the career of Old Brin constituted a pre-emption claim to guardianship, and, if acknowledged by the preceding guardian, the claim could not be jumped so long as it was worked with reasonable diligence.

While Old Brin infested Sierra Valley and vicinity he was my ward, and I regret to say that his conduct was tumultuous and sanguinary in the extreme. I can remember as if it were but yesterday how, one afternoon when Virginia City was deplorably peaceful and local news simply did not exist, Old Brin went on a rampage over toward Sierra Valley and slaughtered two Italian woodchoppers in the most wanton and sensational manner. More than ten years later I met in Truckee an old settler who remembered the painful occurrence well, because the Italians were working for him at the time, and he told me the story to prove that Old Brin had once roamed that part of the mountains. Naturally I was so pleased to learn that my humble effort to keep the local columns of the Virginia Chronicle up to the high standard of frozen truth had not been in vain, that it was with the greatest difficulty I dropped a sympathetic tear when the old settler of Truckee mourned the sad fate of his Italian friends.

If memory be not at fault, it was the episode of the woodchoppers that precipitated the long-cherished design of Virginia City's most noted sportsmen to make a combined effort to secure the pelt of Old Brin and undying glory. About a score of them, heavily armed and provisioned for a month, sallied forth from the Comstock to find and camp upon the trail of the clubfoot bear. They returned without his pelt, but they brought back some picturesque and lurid explanations of their failure and added several chapters to the history of Old Brin.

One of the party was Ned Foster, who never stood to lose on any proposition and never was known to play any game on the square. Being lame, Foster did not have any ambition to meet the big bear, but contented himself with shooting birds for the pot and helping the camp cook. One morning, after all the mighty hunters had gone out on their quest, Foster picked up his shot-gun, jocularly remarked that he guessed he would fetch in a bear, and limped away toward a brushy ridge. Presently the cook heard a shot, followed by yells of alarm, and peering from the tent he saw Foster coming down the slope on a gallop, followed by a monstrous bear. The cook seized a rifle, tried to load it with shot cartridges, and realizing that his agitation made him hopelessly futile, abandoned the attempt to help Foster and scrambled up a tree. From his perch the cook watched with solicitude the progress of Foster and the bear, shouting to Foster excited advice to increase his pace and informing him of gains made by the pursuer.

"Run, Ned! Good Lord, why don't you let yourself out?" yelled the frantic cook, as Foster lost a length on the turn into the home-stretch. "You're not running a lick on God's green earth. The bear's gaining on you every jump, Ned. Turn yourself loose! Ned, you've just got to run to beat that bear!"

Ned went by the tree in a hitch-and-kick gallop, and as he passed he gasped in scornful tones: "You yapping coyote, do you think I'm selling this race!" Perhaps he wasn't, but it looked that way to the man up the tree.

That was the end of the tale as it was told by the Comstockers, who refused to spoil a good climax by gratifying mere idle curiosity about the finish of the race. But Foster was not eaten up by Old Brin--of course his pursuer was the clubfooted bear--and something extraordinary must have happened to save him. An indefinite prolongation of the situation is unthinkable. Wherefore things happened in this wise: Foster's hat fell off, and while the bear was investigating it the man gained a few yards and time enough to climb a stout sapling, growing upon the brink of a cleft in the country rock about a dozen feet wide and twice as deep. The tree was as thick as a man's leg at the base and very tall. Foster climbed well out of reach of the bear, and, perched in a crotch twenty feet above the ground, he felt safe. Old Brin sat down at the foot of the tree, and with head cocked sidewise thoughtfully eyed the man who had affronted him with a charge of small shot. Presently he arose and with his paws grasped the tree ten or twelve feet from the ground, and Foster laughed derisively at the notion of that clumsy beast trying to climb. But Brin had no notion of climbing. Holding his grip, he backed away, and as the tree bent toward him he took a fresh hold higher up, and so, hand over hand, pulled the top of it downward and prepared to pluck Foster or shake him down like a ripe persimmon.

A part of Foster's habitual attire under all circumstances in warm weather was a long linen duster, and it is a defect of ursine perception to confound a man with his clothes. When the napping skirt of Foster's duster seemed to be within reach, the over-eager bear made a grab for it, and released his grasp of the tree. The backward spring of the tough sapling nearly dislodged the clinging man, but it also gave him an idea, and when the grizzly began a repetition of the manoeuvre, he shifted his position a little higher and to the other side.

Old Brin was not appeased by the shred of linen he had secured, and again began bending the sapling over. This time he had to bend it further to get Foster within reach, but the flapping coat-tail again tempted him too soon, and although he secured most of the skirt, he let go his hold and the tree sprang back like a bended bow. Foster let go his hold too in mid-arc and went sailing through the air and across the ravine, landing in a thicket with a jar that loosened his teeth but broke no bones. He said the Grizzly sat bolt upright and looked at the tree, the ravine and him for five minutes, then cuffed himself soundly on both ears and slunk away in evident humiliation and disgust.

\* \* \* \* \*

Nothing but Joe Stewart's flawless reputation for veracity could have induced the Comstock to accept the account of Old Erin's visit to camp, which broke up the trip, as it was given by the hunters when they returned. Mr. Stewart made his living at cards and knew no other profession or trade, but his word was as good as a secured note at the bank, his views on ethical questions were considered superior to a bishop's, and all around he was conceded to be a better citizen and an honester man than Nevada had been able to send to the United States Senate. Therefore, as Joe Stewart was one of the party and did not deny that events happened as described by Col. Orndorff, the Comstock never doubted the story of the Blazing Bear.

This section of the expedition had a large wall tent and all camp conveniences, including lamps and a five-gallon can of kerosene. They pitched their tent upon the bank of a stream near a deep pool such as trout love in warm weather, and they played the national game every night.

Col. Orndorff had opened an opulent jackpot, and Long Brown was thinking about raising before the draw when he felt a nudge at his elbow as if some one had stumbled against him. He was annoyed and he drove his arm backward violently against the canvas, encountering something solid and eliciting a loud and angry snort. Long Brown moved just in time to escape the sweep of a huge paw, armed with claws like sickles, which rent a great gap in the back of the tent and revealed a gigantic bear still sneezing from the blow on the end of his nose and obviously in a nasty temper.

[Illustration: Long Brown moved just in time.]

The poker party went out at the front just as Old Brin came in at the back, and Long Brown thoughtfully took the front pole with him, letting the canvas down over the bear and impeding pursuit. The lamps were broken in the fall, and the oil blazed up under the canvas. Col. Orndorff, Mr. Stewart, Bill Gibson, Doughnut Bill and the cook, Noisy Smith, climbed trees before taking time to see how matters were getting arranged in the tent, and Long Brown stopped at the brink of the pool and turned around to see if the bear was following him.

There was complicated trouble in the tent. The bear had tangled himself in the canvas and was blindly tossing it about, rolling himself up in the slack, and audibly complaining of the fire and smoke. The rifles, shot-guns and all but one revolver had been left in the tent, and presently they began to pop. Doughnut Bill, safe in a sycamore, hitched around to the lee side of the trunk and said: "Mr. Brown, I seriously advise that you emulate the judicious example of the other gentlemen in this game and avoid exposing yourself unnecessarily to such promiscuous and irresponsible shooting as that bear is doing."

"That's dead straight," added Col. Orndorff. "Shin up a tree, Brown, or you'll get plunked."

"Think I'll mix in a little," replied Brown, drawing his gun and opening fire upon the center of the disturbance. A bursting shot gun answered his first shot, and the charge plowed a furrow near Long Brown and threw dirt in his face. Then the cartridge boxes began exploding as the fire reached them, exciting the bear to more tumultuous struggles with the enfolding canvas and louder roars of pain and rage. The five-gallon oil can, probably punctured by Long Brown's bullets, furnished the climax to the volcanic display by blowing up and filling the air with burning canvas, blankets and hardware, and out of the fire and smoke rushed the blazing bear straight toward Long Brown and the creek. Even Long Brown's nerve was not equal to facing a ton of Grizzly headed toward him in a whirlwind of flame. He turned and dove into the pool. That was Old Brin's destination also, and he followed Long Brown with a great splash and a distinct sizzle. Brown swam under water down stream, and the bear went straight across, up the opposite bank and into the brush, howling blue murder.

In the morning, when the fire had burned out, the sportsmen raked over the ruins and recovered the larger part of the jackpot, consisting of gold and silver coins partly fused and much blackened. "Here, gentlemen," said Doughnut Bill, "we have convincing proof of the wisdom of our Pacific Coast statesmen and financiers in retaining metal as a circulating medium during the late lamentable unpleasantness. Had we succumbed to the vicious habit of using paper substitutes for money, we should now be weeping over the ashes of a departed jackpot. Therefore, I suggest that this is an auspicious occasion for passing suitable resolutions reaffirming Nevada's invincible repugnance to a debased currency, her unalterable fidelity to hard money and her distinguished approval of the resumption of specie payment."

"Get in a whack at the Greenbackers," said Col. Orndorff.

"I surely approves the suggestion," said Mr. Stewart. "As a Jacksonian Democrat, I views with alarm the play the Greenbackers make for fusion, which the same is a brace game."

Mr. Gibson also allowed that fusion should be coppered by Nevada, and Noisy Smith whispered his assent, and the resolutions were adopted unanimously.

The disposition of the jackpot was then considered. Col. Orndorff was willing to divide it, but he allowed that if the bear had not butted into the game he would have raked it down to a dead moral certainty.

"I don't know about that," said Doughnut Bill. "The intrusion of our combustible friend was unwarrantable and ungentlemanly, not to say rude, but as the holder of three aces before the draw I claim an interest in the pot. Of course I can't show the cards, but that is the fact. On your honor as the opener of the pot, Colonel, what did you have?"

"Seven full on eights."

"That's good," whispered Noisy Smith. "I had a four flush."

Long Brown put his hand into his pocket, drew forth five water-soaked cards, laid them down and said: "Had 'em in my hand when I dove."

Col. Orndorff looked at them and silently shoved the melted jackpot over to Long Brown. Long Brown's hand was an eight full on sevens.

\* \* \* \* \*

So long as Old Brin was under the guardianship of his early friends, it was certain that no serious harm would come to him and that no hunter would be permitted to boast of having conquered him. But a later breed of journalistic historians, having no reverence for the traditions of the craft and no regard for the truth, sprang up, and the slaughter of the club-footed Grizzly began. His range was extended "from Siskiyou to San Diego, from the Sierra to the sea," and he was encountered by mighty hunters in every county in California and killed in most of them.

Old Clubfoot's first fatal misadventure was in Siskiyou, where he was caught in a trap and shot by two intrepid men, who stuffed his skin and sent it to San Francisco for exhibition at a fair. He had degenerated to a mangy, yellow beast of about 500 pounds weight, with a coat like a wornout doormat, and but for a card labelling him as "Old Reelfoot," and exploiting the prowess of his slayers, his old friends never would have known him.

Clubfoot's first reincarnation took place in Ventura, about 600 miles from the scene of his death. He appeared in a sheep camp at night, sending the herders up the tallest trees in terror, and scattered the flock all over a wide-spreading mountain. The herders spent the best part of a week in gathering the lost sheep, but after the most thorough search of which they were capable, some fifty odd were still missing. When the superintendent came around on his monthly tour of inspection, the herders told him the story of the lost sheep, and he did not know whether to believe it or suspect the herders of illicit traffic in mutton.

Knowing the mountain well, however, and having in mind some places which might easily be overlooked by the herders, the superintendent concluded to make an attempt to clear up the mystery for his own satisfaction. For two or three days he sought in vain for the trail of the missing sheep, visiting several likely places unknown to the herders, and he was about to give up the search when his mind pulled out of a dusty pigeon-hole of memory a faded picture of a queer nook in the mountain, into which he had stumbled many years before in chase of a wounded deer. More for the sake of seeing if he could find the place again than in hope of solving the sheep mystery, he renewed his search, and, at the end of a day's riding over the spurs of the mountain and up and down ravines, he recognized the slope down which he had chased the wounded deer, and saw upon it the hoof prints of sheep not quite obliterated by wind and rain.

At the bottom of the slope was a small flat seemingly hemmed in on three sides by steep walls. At the upper end, however, behind a thick grove of pines, was a break in one of the side walls leading to an enclosed cienega, an emerald gem set deep in the mountain, as though a few acres of ground had sunk bodily some fifty feet, forming a pit in which water had collected and remained impounded until it broke an outlet through the lower wall.

When the superintendent reached the entrance to this sunken meadow, an opening perhaps thirty yards wide, he noticed a well worn path across it from wall to wall, and a glance told him that the path had been beaten by a bear pacing to and fro. Looking closely at this beaten trail, he saw that the footprints were large and that one paw of the bear was malformed. Old Clubfoot without doubt.

Huddled in silent terror close to the farther wall of the little valley were about forty sheep, and near the beaten path were the remains of ten or a dozen carcases. A little study of the situation and the sign told the story to the old mountaineer. The frightened band of sheep, fleeing blindly before the bear, had been driven by chance or by design into this natural trap, and the wily old bear had mounted guard at the entrance and paced his beat until the sheep were thoroughly cured of any tendency to wander down toward the lower end of the meadow. When he wanted mutton, he caught a fat sheep, carried it to his sentry beat and killed and ate it there, leaving the remains as a warning to the rest not to cross the dead line. The grass in the cienega was thick and green, and there was enough seepage of water to furnish drink for the flock. So the provident bear had several months' supply of mutton on the hoof, penned up and growing fat in his private storehouse, and his trail across the entrance was as good as a five-barred gate.

A man less wise than the superintendent would have undertaken to drive the sheep out and back to camp, but the superintendent knew the ways of sheep and foresaw that an attempt to rescue them without the aid of dogs and herders would result only in an endless surging to and fro in the basin. Besides it was almost dusk, the bear might come home to supper at any moment and a revolver was of little use in a bear fight in the dark. Moreover the looting of Old Clubfoot's larder would only ensure more midnight raids on the flocks upon the mountain. Therefore the superintendent rode away.

The next day he returned with an old muzzle-loading Belgian musket of about 75 calibre, a piece of fresh pork and some twine, and he busied himself awhile among some trees near the bear's sentry beat. When he left, the old musket was tied firmly to the tree in such a position that the muzzle could be reached only from in front and in line with the barrel. In the breech of the barrel were ten drams of quick rifle powder, and upon the powder rested a brass 12-gauge shot shell, which had been filled with molten lead. Upon the muzzle was tied the fresh pork, attached to a string tied to the trigger and passing through a screw eye back of the guard. The superintendent knew that pork would be tempting to a mutton-sated bear, and he chuckled as he rode away.

At midnight in the camp upon the mountain the superintendent heard a muffled roar echoing far away, and he laughed softly, turned over and went to sleep. In the morning, with two herders and their collies, he went back to the cienega. There was not much left of the musket, but in front of where it had been was a pool of blood, and a crimson-splashed trail led away from that spot across the flat and down a brushy gulch.

Cautiously, rifle in hand, the superintendent followed the blood sign, urging the unwilling dogs ahead and leading the more unwilling Basque shepherds, who had no stomach for meetings with a wounded grizzly in the brush. Half a mile from the cienega the dogs stopped before a thicket, bristled their backs and growled impatient remonstrance to the superintendent's efforts to shove them into the brush with his foot. In response to urgent encouragement, the collies, bracing back, barked furiously at the thicket, while the herders edged away to climbable trees, and the superintendent waited with tense nerves for the rush of a wounded bear.

But nothing stirred in the thicket, no growl answered the dogs. Five minutes, perhaps--it seemed like half an hour--the superintendent stood there with rifle ready and cold drops beading his forehead. Then he backed away, picked up a stone, and heaved it into the brush. Another and still others he threw until he had thoroughly "shelled the woods" without eliciting a sound or a movement. The silence gave the dogs courage and slowly they pushed into the thicket with many haltings and backward starts, and presently their barking changed in tone and told the man that they had found something of which they were not afraid. Then the superintendent pushed his way through the bushes and found the bear dead. The big slug from the musket had entered his throat and traversed him from stem, to stern, and spouting his life blood in quarts he had gone half a mile before his amazing vitality ebbed clean away and left him a huge heap of carrion.

It is the tradition of the mountain that the ursine shepherd was none other than Old Clubfoot, and it is not worth while to dispute with the faith of a man who follows sheep in the solitudes.

* * * * *

Like Phra the Phoenician, Old Clubfoot could not stay dead, and when there was trouble afoot in the world, with tumult and fighting, no grave was deep enough, no tomb massive enough to hold him. His next recrudescence was in Old Tuolumne, where he forgot former experiences with steel traps and set his foot into the jaws of one placed in his way by vindictive cattlemen. Attached to the chain of the trap was a heavy pine chunk, and Old Clubfoot dragged the clog for many miles, leaving through the brush a trail easily followed, and lay down to rest in a thicket growing among a huddle of rocks.

Hot upon the trail came two hunters, Wesley Wood and a Sclavonian whose name was something like Sakarovitch, and had been simplified to Joe Screech. Wood was certain that the bear had stopped in the thicket, which was almost on the verge of one of the walls of Hetch-Hetchy Valley, a replica of Yosemite on half scale, and he was too old a hand at the game to follow the trail in. One experience with a bear in the brush is enough to teach the greatest fool in the world, if he survives, that wild animals do not lie down to rest without taking precautions against surprise by possible pursuers. They do not stop short in their tracks and go to sleep where any chance comer may walk over them, but make a half circle loop or letter U in the trail and lie where they can watch the route by which they came.

Joe Screech had not learned this, and he jeered at Wood for halting at the thicket. Wood admitted that he was afraid to follow the trail another foot and tried to hold Joe back, but Joe had killed black bears and knew nothing of Grizzlies, and he had a contemptuous opinion of the courage of bears and a correspondingly exalted belief in his own. At least he was afraid somebody might suspect him of being afraid, and he confounded caution with cowardice in others.

So Joe Screech laughed offensively at Wood as he strode into the thicket. "If you're afraid," he said, "you stay there and I'll run the bear out. Maybe you'd better climb a tree."

"That's just what we both would do if we had any sense. Joe Screech, you are the damnedest fool in Tuolumne. That bear'll teach you something if he don't kill you."

"Oh, climb a tree and watch my smoke," and Joe passed out of sight.

Presently Joe's head appeared again as he climbed upon a boulder close to the edge of the cliff and peered around him. A sudden rattling of iron upon stone, a deep growl and a castanet clashing of teeth, and the Grizzly arose behind Joe Screech, towering far above him and swinging the trap from his paw. Joe Screech had time for but one glance of terror, and as he jumped the bear swung trap, chain and clog in the air and reached for him with a mighty blow. It was the fifty-pound steel trap that landed upon Joe's head and sent him plunging over the cliff just as Wood's Winchester began to bark. As fast as the lever could be worked the bullets thudded into the Grizzly's back even while Joe was pitching forward.

Old Clubfoot had ignored the trap and the clog in his eagerness to reach the man with his nearest paw, and the impetus of the stroke, aided by the momentum of the circling clog, threw him from his balance. Probably a bullet in the back of the head had its effect also, for the huge bulk of the bear toppled forward and followed Joe Screech over the cliff.

Wood scrambled desperately through the thicket to the cliff and looked down into Hetch-Hetchey. A thousand feet below, where the talus began to slope from the sheer cliff, dust was still floating, and stones were sliding down a fresh scar in the loose soil of the steep incline toward the forest at the foot.

\* \* \* \* \*

In his old age, the big brindled bear grew weary of being killed and resurrected and longed for a quiet life. Little, ordinary, no-account bears had personated him and got themselves killed under false pretenses from one end of the Sierra to the other, and some of them had been impudent enough to carry their imposture to the extent of placing step-ladders against his sign-board trees and recording their alleged height a yard or two above his mark. That made him tired. Moreover the gout in his bad foot troubled him more and more, and he ceased to get much satisfaction from rolling around on a "flat wheel" and scaring people with his tracks. Wherefore Clubfoot deserted his old haunts and went down into a green valley, inhabited by bee-keepers and other peaceable folk, where he lived on locusts and honey and forgot the strenuous life.

All went well with the retired terror of the mountains for a long time. The only fly in the ointment of his content was Jerky Johnson, who kept dogs and went pirooting around the hills with a gun, making much noise and scaring the wits out of coyotes and jack rabbits. Old Clubfoot realized that his eyes were dimming and his hearing becoming impaired, and it annoyed him to be always on the alert, lest he should come across Jerky in the brush and step on him inadvertently.

Jerky's ostensible occupation, from which his front name was derived, was killing deer and selling jerked venison, but if the greater part of his stock was not plain jerked beef, the cattle-men in that section were victims of strange hallucinations and harborers of nefarious suspicions. Although Clubfoot was credited with large numbers of dead steers found on the ranges, he was conscious of his own innocence, due to some extent to the loss of most of his teeth, and he had better reason than the cow-men had for putting it up to Jerky.

These particulars concerning Mr. Johnson's vocation enable the reader to appreciate the emotions aroused in the breast of Old Clubfoot when he found a newspaper blowing about a bee ranch and saw a thrilling account of his own death at the hands of the redoubtable Jerky Johnson. He had just tipped over a hive and was about to fill up with luscious white sage honey when that deplorably sensational newspaper fluttered under his eye and the scandalous fabrication of Jerky stared him in the face. "This is the limit," he moaned, and his great heart broke.

Slowly and painfully the poor old bear staggered down the valley. His eyes were glazed and he could not tell where the trees and barb-wire fences were until he butted his nose against them. The gout in his maimed foot throbbed horribly, and all the loose bullets in his system seemed to have assembled in his chest and taken the place of his once stout heart. But he had a fixed purpose in his mind, and on he went to its fulfillment, grimly determined to make a fitting finish to a romantic life.

At the lower end of the valley lived the country doctor. To his house came the club-footed bear at midnight, worn and nearly spent with the pitiful journey. There was a dim light in the back office, but it was unoccupied. Clubfoot heaved his bulk against the door and broke the lock, softly entered the room and sniffed anxiously of the rows of jars and bottles upon a shelf. His eyes were dim and he could not read the labels, but his nose was still keen and he knew he should find what he was seeking. He found it. Taking down a two-gallon jar, Clubfoot tucked it under his arm tenderly and walked out erect, just as in the old days he was wont to walk away from a farmyard with a calf or a pig under each arm. It has been said of him that he could carry off a steer in that fashion, but probably that is an exaggeration or even a fable.

Behind the doctor's stable was a bucket containing the sponge used in washing the doctor's carriage. Clubfoot found the bucket, broke the two-gallon jar upon the sharp edge and spilled the contents upon the sponge. Taking one last look at the stars and the distant mountain peaks, he plunged his muzzle into the sponge, jammed his head tightly into the bucket and took one long, deep breath.

In the morning "Doc." Chismore found a gigantic dead bear behind the barn, with the stable bucket firmly fixed upon his head and covering his nose and mouth. Scattered about were the fragments of a chloroform jar, and between the claws of the bear's maimed foot was a crumpled Sunday supplement of a yellow journal, containing an account of the slaying of Old Brin, the Club-footed Grizzly, by Jerky Johnson. Being a past master of woodcraft, Doctor Chismore read the signs like a printed page, and applying the method of Zadig he reconstructed the whole story of the dolorous passing of the greatest bear in the world.

## CHAPTER IV: MOUNTAIN CHARLEY.

Charles McKiernan was a well-known lumber merchant of San

Jose, Cal. To old timers he was "Mountain Charlie," having spent most of his life in the Santa Cruz mountains, where he owned timber land and saw mills. McKiernan's face was strangely disfigured. His left eye was missing and his forehead was so badly scarred that he wore his hair in a bang falling to his eyebrows to conceal the marks. From his own lips I heard the story of those scars.

This was also in the days of the muzzle-loading rifle. McKiernan and a partner were holding down timber claims in the mountains and living in a cabin overlooking a wide canyon. One morning they saw a Grizzly turning over rocks at the foot of a spur jutting from the main ridge into the canyon, and taking their rifles they followed the ridge around to the spur to get a shot at him from that point. It so happened that the bear also fancied that he had business on the top of the spur, and began climbing soon after the men lost sight of him.

The bear and the men met unexpectedly at the top, and the bear halted hesitatingly with his head and breast just showing above the rocks at the brink of the steep slope. McKiernan did not want to begin the fight at such close quarters, and he was confident that the bear would back down and attempt to return to the brush at the foot of the spur if given time. Then he would have the advantage of the up-hill position and plenty of time to reload if the bear should attempt to return after the first shot.

But McKiernan's partner lost his nerve, turned tail and ran away, and that encouraged the bear to take the offensive, just as it would invite attack from a hesitating dog. The Grizzly sprang up over the edge of the steep and charged McKiernan, who threw up his rifle and fired at the bear's chest. It was a Yeager rifle carrying an ounce ball, and it checked the charge for a moment by bringing the bear to his knees. As the bear gathered himself for another rush, McKiernan swung the heavy rifle and struck the bear over the head with the barrel. He was a powerful man, accustomed to swinging an axe, and the blow knocked the bear down and stunned him. The stock of the rifle broke in McKiernan's hands and the barrel fell close by the bear, which had fallen upon the very edge of a steep slope at the side of the spur or knob.

McKiernan stooped to recover the rifle barrel with which to beat the bear to death, and in doing so his head came close to the bear's. The Grizzly had partly recovered, and throwing his head upward he closed his jaws upon McKiernan's forehead, with a snap like a steel trap. One lower tusk entered the left eye socket, and an upper canine tooth sunk into the skull. McKiernan fell face downward, his arms under his face, and the bear slid over the edge and rolled down the almost vertical wall into the canyon, having dislodged himself by the effort to seize the man.

McKiernan did not lose consciousness, but he was unable to move. He knew his left eye was gone, and he feared that he was bleeding to death. He heard the bear rolling down the slope, heard the crash of bushes as he struck the bottom, and knew because of his bawling that the Grizzly was mortally hurt. Then he wondered why his partner did not come to him, and sense of pain and fear of death were submerged under a wave of indignation at the man's cowardice and flight. Presently he heard faintly a voice calling him across the canyon, but could not distinguish the words, and after a time he realized that his partner had fled back to the cabin, and was shouting to him. He could not answer, nor could he raise his head, but he managed to free one arm and wave it feebly. The partner finally saw the movement and plucked up enough courage to come back, and with his help McKiernan somehow got to the cabin.

A young doctor from San Jose attempted to patch up the broken skull after removing a large piece and leaving the envelope of the brain exposed. He had read something about trephining and inserting silver plates, and he hammered out a silver dollar and set it like a piece of mosaic into McKiernan's forehead, where it resisted the efforts of nature to repair damages and caused McKiernan a thousand times more agony than he had suffered from the Grizzly's tusks. Only the marvelous vitality of the man saved him from the consequences of such surgery. For days and weeks he sat in his cabin dripping his life away out of a wound that closed, swelled with fierce pain and broke out afresh, and the drain upon his system gave him an incredible appetite for meat, which he devoured in Gargantuan quantities.

Then old Doctor Spencer went up to "Mountain Charlie's" cabin, took out the silver dollar, removed a wad of eyebrow that had been pushed into the hole made by the bear's lower tooth in the eye socket, and McKiernan recovered.

And the first thing he did when he was able to travel was to load up a shotgun and hunt San Jose from one end to the other for the man who had set a silver dollar in his skull.

## CHAPTER V: IN THE VALLEY OF THE SHADOW.

Over-confidence and some contempt for bears, born of easy victories cheaply won, led one noted Californian hunter into The Valley of the Shadow, from which he emerged content to let his fame rest wholly upon his past record and without ardor for further distinction as a slayer of Grizzlies. As mementoes of a fight that has become a classic in the ursine annals of California, John W. Searles, the borax miner of San Bernardino, kept for many years in his office a two-ounce bottle filled with bits of bone and teeth from his own jaw, and a Spencer rifle dented in stock and barrel by the teeth of a Grizzly.

On a hunting trip in Kern county, Mr. Searles had a remarkable run of luck and piled three bears in a heap without moving out of his tracks or getting the least sign of fight. It was so easy that he insisted upon going right through the Tehachepi range and killing all the Grizzlies infesting the mountains. He and his party made camp in March, 1870, not far from the headquarters of General Beale's Liebra ranch in the northern part of Los Angeles county. Romulo Pico was then in charge at the Liebra, and nearly thirty years later, while hunting a notorious bear on the scene of Searles's adventure, he told me the story of the fight.

Searles was armed with a Spencer repeater but had shot away the ammunition adapted to the rifle and had been able to procure only some cartridges which fitted the chamber so badly that two blows of the hammer were generally required to explode one of them. Notwithstanding this serious defect of his weapon, Searles had so poor an opinion of the Grizzly that he went out alone after the bear several miles from camp. There was some snow on the ground and on the brush, and finding bear tracks, Searles tied his horse and took the trail afoot. He found a bear lying asleep under the brush and killed it, and while he was standing over the body he heard another bear breaking brush in a thicket not far away.

Leaving the dead bear, he took up the trail of its mate and followed until his clothing was soaked with melting snow and the daylight was almost gone. The bear halted in a dense thicket and Searles began working his way through the chaparral to stir him up. Of course the bear was not where his tracks seemed to indicate him to be, and the meeting was sudden and unexpected. The bear rose within two feet of the hunter and almost behind him. There was neither time nor room to put rifle to shoulder, and Searles swung it around, pointed it by guess and fired. The ball did little damage, but the powder flash partly blinded the bear and it came down to all-fours and began pawing at its eyes, giving Searles an opportunity to throw in another cartridge and take fair aim at the head.

If Searles had not forgotten in his excitement the defect of his weapon, the bear fight would have been ended right there. He pulled trigger with deadly aim, but the rifle missed fire. Instead of re-cocking the piece and trying a second snap, he worked the lever, threw in a new cartridge and pulled the trigger. Again no explosion. Again he failed to remember the trick of the rifle, and tried a third cartridge, which also missed fire.

Then the bear became interested in the affair and turned upon the hunter at close quarters. Seizing the barrel of the rifle in his jaws, the Grizzly wrenched it from Searles's grasp, threw it aside and hurled himself bodily upon his foe. Searles went down beneath the bear. Placing one paw upon his breast the bear crunched the hunter's lower jaw between his teeth, tore a mouthful of flesh from his throat and took a third bite out of his shoulder. Then he rolled the man over, bit into his back and went away.

The cold Californian night saved the man's life by freezing the blood that flowed from his wounds and sealing up the torn veins. He was a robust, hardy man, and he pulled himself together and refused to die out there in the brush. With his jaw hanging by shreds, his wind-pipe severed and his left arm dangling useless, he crawled to his horse, got into the saddle and rode to camp, whence his companions took him to the Liebra ranch house. Romulo Pico was sure Searles would die before morning, but he dressed the wounds with the simple skill of the mountaineer who learns some things not taught in books, and tried to make death as little painful as possible. Finding Searles not only alive in the morning but obstinately determined not to submit to the indignity of being killed by a bear, Pico hitched up a team to a ranch wagon and sent him to Los Angeles, a two-days' journey, where the surgeons consulted over him and proposed all sorts of interesting operations by way of experiment upon a man who was sure to die anyway.

Searles was unable to tell the surgeons what he thought of their schemes for wiring him together, but he indicated his dissent by kicking one of them in the stomach. Then they called in a dentist as an expert on broken jaws, after they had attended to the other damages, and the dentist showed them how to remove the debris and where to patch and sew, and they managed to get the shattered piece of human machinery tinkered up in fairly good shape. The vitality and obstinacy of Searles did the rest, and in a few weeks he was on his feet again and planning prospecting trips to Death Valley, not The Valley of the Shadow through which he had passed, but the grewsome desert of Southern California where he found his fortune in borax.

## CHAPTER VI: WHEN GRIZZLIES RAN IN DROVES.

William Thurman, who owned a lumber mill on the Chowchilla mountain, not far from the Mariposa grove of Big Trees, told this plain, unadorned tale of an old-fashioned Grizzly bear hunt.

He was moved thereto by inspection of a Winchester express rifle, carrying a half-inch ball, backed by 110 grains of powder, that was shown to him by a hunter.

"If we had been armed with such rifles in early days," said Mr. Thurman, "the Grizzly wouldn't have achieved his reputation for vitality and staying powers in a fight. There is no doubt that he is a very tough animal and a game fighter, but in the days when he made a terrible name for himself he had to face no such weapons as that.

"I assisted in killing, in 1850, the first Grizzlies that were brought into the town of Sonora. I had heard a great deal about the Grizzly, and coming across the plains I talked to my comrade, Green, about what I should do if I should get a chance at a bear. I was a pretty good shot, and thought it would be no trick at all to kill a bear with the Mississippi rifle that I brought home from the Mexican war.

"One day I went out with a man named Willis, who was a good hunter, and in the hills back of Sonora we found plenty of bear sign. In fact we could get through the thick brush and chaparral only on the trails made by bears, and we had to go carefully for fear of running upon a Grizzly at close quarters. Although it was evident that we were in a bear country, we hadn't seen anything to shoot at when we emerged from the brush into an open space about fifty yards in diameter.

"Willis said that he was sure bears were close around us, if we could only see them, and I proposed to climb a tree on the other side of the clearing and get a good view of the surrounding thickets. If I should see bears I was to make a noise and try to scare them out of their hiding places.

"I started across the opening, but before I reached the tree I saw a huge Grizzly coming toward me through the brush. He looked much larger and uglier than I had expected, and it struck me that the proper thing for me was to get into that tree before shooting. I got to the tree all right enough, but found that I couldn't climb it and take my rifle up with me. Willis saw my difficulty and shouted to me that I couldn't make it, and so I abandoned the attempt and ran back toward him.

"The bear was following me, and Willis started back into the brush. I called to him not to do that, but to stand in the open and wait for me. He halted, and when I got alongside we both turned and raised our rifles. When the bear saw that we were standing our ground, he stopped, looked at us a moment and then turned and shuffled back into the brush. He was so big and looked so formidable that we concluded to let him go unmolested, rather relieved, in fact, that we were let out of the scrape so easily.

"We made our way back to camp with some caution and decided that we would get up a crowd and go bear hunting the next day. When we told our adventure, Green was very hilarious at my expense and kept reminding me of the brave things I had said coming across the plains. He was so everlastingly tickled with his joke that he sat up all that night to guy me about my running away from a bear. I told him I would show him all the bears he wanted to see the next day, and give him a chance to try his own nerves.

"The next day five of us went out to look for bears, and we struck them thick before we got to the place where we had found so much sign. Willis and I took the upper side of a patch of brush, and Green and the other two skirted the lower edge. An old Grizzly and two cubs, startled by some noise made by the other fellows, jumped out of the brush on our side, and we fired at them. My bullet struck one near the shoulder, and Willis hit the dam in the belly. They all turned and ran down through the brush toward the rest of the crowd, and got out of our range.

"The noise made by them in running through the brush stirred up another squad, and when the shooting began down below five bears came tearing out on our side to get out of the way. Willis raised his rifle and pulled the trigger, but luckily the cap failed to explode. The five turned as soon as they saw us and ran in another direction. I was going to shoot one in the rump, but Willis stopped me, saying that we had our hands full without inviting any more bears to join the scrimmage. Before those five bears, got out of sight three more broke cover and joined them, and for a moment there were eleven Grizzly bears, young and old, in sight from where I stood. Eight of them ran away and the original three kept us all busy for the best part of the afternoon.

"For some time the other three men had all the fun, while Willis and I stood guard on our side of the thicket and watched the performance. The old bear would stand up and look over a patch of brush to locate her enemy, and somebody would give her a shot. She would drop to all fours and gallop around to where she saw the man last, and he would run around the other side and reload. The cubs were half grown--big enough to be dangerous--and the boys had to watch for them while dodging about.

"I got even on Green that afternoon. He had forgotten to bring any caps, and after his first shot he could do nothing but dodge around the brush and keep out of the way. One of the bears was after him, and he had to step lively. While he was waiting to see which way the bear was coming next, he made motions with his hand, pointing to the nipple of his rifle, to indicate that he wanted caps. I saw what he meant, but instead of going to him to supply him with caps I stood still and laughed at him and applauded his running when the bear chased him. That made him furious and he yelled that if he had a cap he'd take a shot at me.

"After two or three hours of dodging about, every man taking a shot whenever he got a chance, one of the cubs keeled over and the dam and the other cub retreated into the thickest part of the brush patch.

"We consulted and decided that if we killed the other cub next the dam might quit and get away, whereas if we killed the dam the cub probably wouldn't leave her and we'd bag the whole outfit. One of the party crawled cautiously into the thicket and presently he fired. Then he called to me to come in, and when I crawled up to him he said: 'I've killed the cub by mistake, but the old one is lying badly wounded on the other side of a little open spot, and you can get a splendid shot at the butt of her ear while I back out and reload."

"He backed out, and I crawled up and took his place. There was the old bear about ten yards away, lying down and bleeding from a great many wounds. She seemed to be nearly exhausted and out of breath. I was in the act of raising my rifle to take aim at her head, when she caught sight of me and suddenly sprang up and rushed at me. She was almost upon me in two jumps, and I thought I was in for a bad time of it. I had no time to aim, but pushed out my rifle instinctively and fired in her face. The bullet struck her in the mouth, and the pain caused her to stop, wheel around and make a rush through the chaparral in the opposite direction. Such a shot as that from a Winchester express would have blown off the whole roof of her head, but my bullet, as I found later, tore through her tongue, splitting the root, and stopped when it struck bone.

"When she broke out of the brush on the other side three of the boys fired into her and she fell dead. We looked her over and found more than thirty bullets in her. We had been shooting at her and dodging her in the brush from 11 o'clock in the forenoon; until after 3 o'clock, and she had caved in from sheer exhaustion and loss of blood, not from the effects of any single bullet.

"We packed the three carcases into Sonora that night and a butcher named Dodge offered to cut them up and sell the meat without charge to us if we would let him have the bears at his shop. That was the first bear meat ever taken into Sonora, and everybody in the camp wanted a piece. In the morning there was a line of men at Dodge's shop like the crowd waiting at a theatre for Patti tickets. Men far down the line shouted to Dodge not to sell the meat in big pieces, but to save slices for them. The meat sold for $1 a pound. Everybody got a slice, and we got $500 for our three bears.

"One of our crowd was so elated over the profits of bear-hunting that he started out alone the next day to get more Grizzly meat. He didn't come back, and the boys who went out to look for him found his body, covered up with leaves and dirt, in the edge of a clump of brush. His skull had been smashed by a blow from a Grizzly's paw."

# CHAPTER VII: THE ADVENTURES OF PIKE.

Pike was one of the oldest of Yosemite guides and altogether the quaintest of the many queer old fellows who drifted into the valley in early days and there were stranded for life. He had another name, no doubt, but nobody knew or cared what it might be, and he seemed to have forgotten it himself. "Pike" fitted him, served all the purposes for which names were invented, was easy to pronounce, and therefore was all the name he needed. Pike was tall, round-shouldered, lop-sided, slouchy, good-natured, illiterate, garrulous, frankly vain of the little scraps of botanical nomenclature he had picked up and as lazy and unacquainted with soap as an Indian.

Pike dearly loved bears and bear stories. When there were no tourists about to whom he could tell bear stories, he would go into the woods and have adventures with bears and stock up with stories for the next season. Pike never had to kill a bear to get a story out of him. He brought in no bear skins, pointed out no bullet holes, exhibited no scars and told no blood-curdling tales of furious combat and hair-breadth escapes. Pike and the bears appeared to have an understanding that there was room enough in the woods for both and that his hunting was all in the way of innocent amusement and recreation, to be spiced now and then with a practical joke.

"Black bears and brown bears are peaceable folks," Pike used to say in his Californianized-Missourian vernacular. "There's nothing mean about 'em and they don't go around with chips on their shoulders. I generally get along with them slick as grease and they never try to jump me when I haven't got a gun. Why, sir, I can just talk a brown bear out of the trail, even when he thinks he owns it. I did one night in the valley. I was going from Barnard's up to the Stoneman when I ran right up against a big brown bear in the dark. He was coming down the road and was in pretty considerable of a hurry, too--going down to the butcher's corral for supper I reckon--and we stopped about three feet apart. 'What you adoin' of here,' says I. 'Seems to me you're prowling around mighty permiscuous, buntin' inter people on the State stage road. You git inter the bresh,' says I, 'where you belong or I'll kick a few dents into you. Now don't stand here argifying the pint,' says I, just as important as if I was the Gardeen of the Valley, which I wasn't. 'Scoot, skedaddle, vamoos the ranch, git off the earth,' I says, 'if you ain't aimin' to git your head punched.'

"Well, sir, he stood there a minute with his head cocked sidewise, kinder grunted once as if he was saying 'good-night,' and turned off the road into the brush and went about his business, and I poked along up to the Stoneman. 'Course I can't swear that he knew just what I said, but he ketched the general drift of the argyment all right, what you might call the prepoort of my remarks, and he knowed he hadn't no case worth fighting about.

"I remember once when Jim Duncan and me was ketched out in a snowstorm up near the head of Alder Creek, and lost each other in the dark. I knew Jim would take care of himself and it was no use tramping around, so I hunted a hole to sleep in. I found a place under a rock just big enough for me, where the snow didn't blow in, and I curled up on some dry leaves and snoozed off in no time. By and by something touched my face and I woke up, and there was a bear poking his head in and wondering if there was room for two. There wasn't no room and I don't like to sleep with bears nohow. Bears are all right in their place and I don't hold to no prejudices, but I'm notional about some things and I never could stand bears in my bed; they smell worse than Indians. So I says to that bear, which was looking mighty wishful into my snug quarters, 'Git along out of this; I was here first,' and I reached up and fetched him a back-handed slap on the nose. You'd orter heard him sneeze as he moseyed off. Last thing I remembered when I turned over and went to sleep was him a sneezing as he wandered around looking for another hole.

"If that had been a she-bear, of course I'd have crawled out and gave her my place like a gentleman. You never know what a she--bear, or any other kind of she, is going to do next, and the best way to get along with 'em is to let 'em have their own way and be polite. I'm always polite to ladies--or most always any way. Of course when they get too cantankerous a man has to forget his manners and call 'em down.

"I was impolite to a she-bear once, but she got back at me. I was over on the far side of Signal Peak hunting gray squirrels with a shot-gun. I heard a funny sort of squealing a little way off, and set out to find out what was going on in the woods. Poking quietly through the brush, I came to the top of a ledge that dropped off straight and smooth to a flat covered with bear clover, just an opening in the forest. A she-bear was busy cracking open sugar pine cones and showing two cubs how to get the nuts out of them. The little fellows were having a gay old time, wrestling, boxing, stealing nuts from mamma and rolling about in the clover like a couple of kids, and I laid down in some bushes on top of the ledge and watched them. Sometimes they would grab a cone from the old one or bite her ear, and she would scold them and cuff them until thcy yelped that they'd be good. They couldn't be good half a minute, and they had the old lady's patience most worn out before I took a hand in the frolic.

"The old bear's coat was pretty thin and rusty, and she'd been sitting down or coasting down a bear slide so much that all the hair was worn off her hams slick and smooth. She looked mighty ridiculous when her back was turned, and it came into my fool head that a charge of small shot in the smooth place would be mighty surprising to her and help out the fun a whole lot. She couldn't get at me on the ledge, so I was perfectly safe to play jokes on her, and I wanted to see her jump. So I shoved the gun out through a bush and turned it loose. She was sixty yards away and the shot stung her good without doing any great harm.

"'Woof!' said the old bear as she jumped four feet high, and when she lit she was as mad as a wet hen. She looked up at the ledge, but couldn't see me, and she looked all around for somebody or something to blame for her trouble. Not a thing was in sight to account for it. She sat down sort of sideways, reached around with one paw to scratch where it hurt and thought the matter over. I had to stuff grass in my mouth to keep from howling with laughter at the way she cocked her head and seemed to be sizing up the situation while she scratched the stinging place.

"The cubs had stopped playing at the sound of the gun and run up close to her, and they were watching her for further orders. The old girl finally got her eye on them, and she looked at them solemnly for half a minute, and it was plain as print she was beginning to have suspicions. Then she was sure she had the thing figured out, and she fetched first one and then the other a cuff that sent them rolling ten feet away. When they got up bawling she was right there and gave them the darndest spanking two innocent cubs ever got. Every time she hit one he would go heels over head and yell blue murder, and by the time he got up she gave him another belt, scolding like an old woman all the time. It seemed to me I could almost hear her say, 'Play tricks on your mammy, will ye? I'll teach ye. Get along home without your supper, ye little scamps, and take that.' And so she went through the woods; spanking her babies, and they a'yelling for keeps and not knowing what they were being licked for, and I rolled around on top of the ledge, kicking my heels in the air and just bellowing with laughter.

"I thought that was the end of the funniest time I ever had with a bear, but it wasn't. Along about the first of March there was a warm spell in the mountains, and I went down the South Fork to Devil's Gulch, which heads up toward Signal Peak, to look over a timber claim and see if it was worth taking up. It was one of those warm days that take the snap out of a man, and I got tired and went to sleep under a tree. When I waked a bear had me half covered up with leaves and was piling on more. I wasn't cold, and didn't need any covering, but she seemed to think I did, and I reckoned the best thing to do was to keep still and let her finish the job. She seemed so serious about it that I didn't dare take it as a joke and try any tricks on her, but I couldn't figure out what her game was. She covered me with oak leaves, pine-needles and dirt from head to foot, and then all was still. I couldn't see, and I didn't dare to lift my head and shake off the leaves.

"After a while I made up my mind to take some chances to find out if the bear was on watch, and I wiggled my foot. Nothing happened, so I wiggled it a little harder. Then I felt around slowly until I got hold of my gun, and when I had that where I could handle it, I jumped up and shook the leaves and dirt from my face. The bear was gone. I had a sort of notion of what she was driving at, and so I fixed up the pile of leaves just as she had left them, went up the hill a little way and shinned a tree.

"About half an hour later the bear came back, leading two half-grown cubs so thin you could count their slats, and I recognized the interesting family I had met and had fun with in the fall. She was saying things to them in bear-talk, sort of whining and grunting, and they wobbled along behind her up to that pile of leaves. The cubs laid down with their tongues hanging out as if they were pretty tired, and the old girl tackled the pile confidently. It was plain enough that she had cached me for dinner, gone home into the gulch after the cubs and brought them back to have a square meal after being holed up for two or three months.

"The old bear made only two or three dabs at the pile when she began to suspect something was wrong, and then she sailed into it like a steam shovel. She made leaves and dirt fly so fast out between her hind legs that the cubs had to get out of the way or be buried, and the more she dug, the more excited she got. She worked over that pile and all the ground for ten feet around it until she was down to the frost, and when she finally got it through her head that the cupboard was bare, she was the most foolish-looking critter a man ever saw. She stood there blinking at the cubs, who were sniffing at the rubbish she had scattered about, and couldn't explain to them what had become of that square meal, and I reckon the cubs had it put up that mamma was getting light-headed and having dreams. They quit prospecting and sat down and looked at her and whined, and that set her off again raking over all the leaves in the neighborhood as if she hoped to find me hiding under them. Pretty soon she struck some kind of a root that was good to eat, and she braced up and called the cubs and showed it to 'em as if that was what she had been hunting for all the time. She made more fuss over that root than there was any call for and pretended it was the greatest thing a bear ever struck in the woods, and the cubs were so glad to get anything that they allowed roots were good enough and forgot all about what she had promised them.

"If her pelt had been good and the cubs had been big enough, I reckon I'd have got even with her for caching me, but she wasn't worth skinning and the cubs were no good for grub. It was getting late and I was tired of my tree, so I ploughed up the dirt under her nose with a load of shot and let out a yell, and she herded those cubs off into the brush and lit out for Devil's Gulch, and I went home. That was the nearest I ever came to being eaten up by bears."

## CHAPTER VIII: IN THE BIG SNOW.

The winter of 1889-90 is memorable in California as the winter of "the big snow." In the latter part of January the Central Pacific line over the Sierra Nevada was blockaded, and three or four passenger trains were imprisoned in the drifts for more than two weeks. Passing through the blockade and over the range afoot, I walked at times above the tops of the telegraph poles, and think it no exaggeration to estimate the depth of snow at the higher altitudes at 25 feet. Drifts in the canyons must have been more than double the depth of the snow on a level. The storm was general and the snowfall throughout the mountain region was extraordinary, not only for quantity but for rapidity. It can snow more inches to the hour in the high Sierra than feet to the week anywhere else, and the big storm of 1890 broke all previous records.

Miners' cabins in the gulches and hunters' shacks on the mountains were buried in a night and the occupants had to tunnel their way out. Deer fled from the slopes down into secluded glens which had been their safe refuge from Sierra storms before, but the white death followed them and softly folded its feathery wings about them. In the spring the dead deer were found in hundreds where they had "yarded" safely through many winters before the big snow. Warm weather before the storm had brought the bears out of their holes and set them to foraging for grub. The snow fell lightly and no crust formed for some time, and bruin could not wallow through it. The best he could do was to get under the lee of a log or ledge, take another nap and nurse his inconvenient appetite. Being a philosopher, bruin did the best he could and trusted the god of the wild things to do the rest.

Upon the long western slope of a big sprawling mountain in Sierra county a Grizzly dam and two gaunt cubs of the vintage of '89 were caught in the big snow miles away from the deep gulch in which they had passed the winter. No doubt that dam was weatherwise enough to sense the coming storm in time to have returned to the den, but neither beast nor man could have guessed what a thick blanket of white the gray clouds were about to lay upon the land. When the flakes began to fall thickly Mother Grizzly quit digging roots and turning over rocks, and sought shelter. The long slope was smooth and bare, but down near the foot was a fallen pine with upturned roots, and into the hollow where the roots had been, under the lee of the matted mass of fibre and dirt, Mother Grizzly led her babies and there made her bed for the night. It was a longer night than the old bear expected. It lasted until the next day's westering sun made a pale, bluish glimmer through the upper part of the drift that covered the fallen tree and filled up the hollow. The warmth of their bodies had kept an open space around the bears, and the upturned roots of the pine had prevented the snow from piling high directly over them, while causing it to drift and form an enclosing barrier in front of the shallow pit made by the uprooting of the tree. Mother Grizzly arose and struggled toward the dim glimmer of light, but she could not break her way out. The snow was light and dry and would not pack, and her buffetings only brought a feathery smother down upon her and the cubs. All she accomplished was to let down the frail roofing of the den and get a glimpse of the sky. She tried to climb up the drift, but sank out of sight and had to back out of the smother. Digging was futile, for the snow offered scarcely more resistance than foam.

So Mother Grizzly gave up her attempt to escape and busied herself with making the hollow as comfortable as possible for a long stay. She scraped down to the dirt and packed the snow about the sides of the lair, stowed the cubs against the back of the den and curled herself in front of them and waited for better times to come.

It is a proverb of the Spaniards that "who sleeps, dines," and bears attest its truth, for it is their experience through the long, cold weeks of winter, when the snow is deep and no food is to be got at. Doubtless the old she bear was content to go to sleep again and forget her hunger, but it may be supposed that the cubs had not learned the philosophy of necessity, and kept her awake with fretful demands which she could not satisfy. Had the family remained holed up in the winter den and not been tempted out by mild weather to break the long fast, probably the desire for food would have remained dormant, but the taste of food awakened appetite, and exercise sharpened it and created insistent necessity for its satisfaction. The normal period of hibernation having passed, dreams were no longer acceptable substitutes for dinner. So the hungry, worrying cubs would not let their dam sleep, and she soon became as ravenous as they and impatient of imprisonment.

Every day Mother Grizzly tried the barrier to find a way out, but for more than two weeks the snow was without a crust that would sustain the weight of a dog, and she could only flounder into the drift a few feet and struggle out again. Then a light drizzle of rain came, and the next night there was a sharper tingle in the air, a promise of cold weather, and crust began to form. In a day or two more it would be firm enough to travel upon, and the old Grizzly would lead her starving cubs down into the foothills and hunt for a stray calf or a sheep with which to feed them.

The big snow obliterated mountain roads and trails, and the mail was carried to many of the smaller mountain settlements by men on snowshoes, who took the shortest feasible routes and found smooth traveling a dozen or fifteen feet above the rough, rock-strewn ground. A Sierra carrier on skis--the long, wooden Norwegian snowshoes-- with a letter pouch strapped to his shoulders, was tempted by the light crust to leave the ridge and shorten his journey by making a cut-off down the long, smooth slope. A minute's swift rush down that slope would save hours of weary plodding above the heads of the gulches.

The carrier studied the stretch of gleaming white carefully to select his course, and determined on a line passing a little below the roots of the fallen pine, which were indicated by a slight fold in the blanket of snow. Setting his steel-shod staff under his left arm pit to serve as brake and rudder and throwing his weight upon it, the carrier ranged his skis parallel, the right in advance a few inches, fixed his attention upon the range mark he had chosen, gave a slight push with the staff and got under way. The crust bore his weight easily, and in two seconds he was gliding swiftly. In five seconds more he was speeding like an arrow from the bow, and the ringing of the steel staff point against the crust arose in a high clear note above the grating sound of the sliding skis.

Mother Grizzly heard the strange sound, which was unlike anything of which she knew the meaning, and cuffing the whining cubs into instant silence, she started cautiously up the barrier to see what was going on or what danger menaced. Her frequent attempts to get out of the hole had made an inclined trench, which came to the surface a few yards from the protruding tree roots, and when she reached the upper end and put her head above the crust she saw a man rushing down the mountain straight toward her with the speed of a falling stone.

The green glint came into the grizzly's eyes, her teeth clashed together in quick, sharp strokes, like the chattering of a chilled bather, and she lunged forward and upward to meet the charge. If the man saw her at all, it was too late to swerve from his course or swing his staff forward for a weapon. His right ski passed under the bear's foreleg and he flew headlong over her, hurtled through the air and crashed through the snow crust a dozen yards beyond her. One of the skis was broken and torn from his foot, and even if his leg had not been broken he would have been helpless where he fell.

Mother Grizzly and the starving cubs broke their fast, and two or three days later they went away over the frozen snow to the foothills. The men who went out in search of the missing carrier, and followed his trail to the fallen pine, brought back the mail pouch and something in a grain sack. They told me what they found, but it was not a pleasing tale and it is best that it be not retold.

## CHAPTER IX: BOSTON'S BIG BEAR FIGHT.

A small party of hunters sat by a campfire in a tamarack grove in the high Sierra. Their guide was William Larkin, Esq., alias "Old Bill," a man who had lived in the mountains for forty years and learned many things worth telling about. A new Winchester rifle that was being cleaned was the immediate provocation of some reminiscent remarks on the subject of pump-guns.

"We old mossbacks are slow to see anything good in new contraptions," said Mr. Larkin, after begging a Turkish cigarette from the Dude and lighting it with the Dude's patent pocket lamp, "but I'm just beginning to get it socked home into my feeble old intellect that things ain't naturally no account just because I never seen 'em afore. I stuck to it for a good many years that an old muzzle-loading rifle was the best shooting tool that ever was or ever could be made, but an old she-bear with one of my bullets through her lungs taught me different by clawing all the clothes and half the meat off my back. I'm learning' slowly, and I ain't too old to learn some more. If I live long enough I'll know consid'able yit.

"I remember the first pump-gun that came into these mountains. It was a Henry sixteen-shooter, and it blew in along with a kid from Boston who wanted to kill a bear. The young chap's uncle tried to convince him that killing a California Grizzly was not as much fun as some folks pretended, but the Boston boy couldn't be convinced, and so the uncle hired me to go along and take care of him. Boston had a gun in a case, and I told him to keep it there until we got to my bear pasture. The rest of his outfit was 500 cartridges and a box of paper collars.

"When we got into camp over on the South Fork, Boston wanted to begin the slaughter right away and opened up that gun case. I'd heard of the repeating rifle, but had it put up for a Yankee lie, and when the boy pulled out the gun I thought he had made a mistake and brought along some scientific contrivance from his college. He told me it was a Henry rifle and showed me how it worked, but I had no use for it. While he stuffed his pump-gun I smoked and thought. 'Unless you go slow, Mr. Larkin,' says I to myself, 'you'll get into plenty of trouble. Here you are, mixed up with something that you don't sabe pretty well. A rough canyon, two hound dogs and an able-bodied bear is a combination that you can work, but when you throw in a college boy and a gun that winds up like a clock and shoots till the cows come home, the situation looks kind of misty.' I didn't think much of the pump-gun, but for all I knew it might go off at both ends and paw up everything by the roots, and I was tolerable sure that Boston would wobble it around so's to take in a pretty consid'able scope of outdoors. But I allowed I was old fashioned enough to circumvent a Boston boy and his new gun, and concluded to go ahead.

"Next morning we put the dogs into Devil's Gulch, and by making a cut over a spur we got about two miles below them and sat down to wait for bear. The trees were so tall and so close together that you couldn't see the tops and the sun never saw the ground. The canyon was narrow and the sides were so steep that they tucked under at the bottom. While we sat there I figured a bit on what was going to happen. There was a light breeze, and presently I noticed something on the other side of the canyon, about fifty yards away. The wind swayed some bushes that grew around a charred stump, and from time to time the black end of the stump showed up and then disappeared very much like a bear's head peeping out of the brush.

"Pretty soon the dogs made a row up the gulch, and as the howls and yells and promiscuous uproar came nearer I knew they had started a bear and made him get a wiggle on. Boston danced around in great excitement, and when I pointed to the black stump he was ready to see bears most anywhere. 'You take care of that,' says I, 'and I'll go and see what ails the dogs.' He opened fire on the stump, and I dodged from tree to tree up the gulch until I was out of range.

"I never was in a battle, but if they made any more noise at Bull Run than Boston was making, I'm glad I wasn't there. I thought I was running away from the biggest fight on record. It was what our military authors call 'a continual roll of musketry.' But while running away from one battle I piled into another and had all the fight I needed on my hands. The dogs and two bears were mixed up in some sort of disagreement about things in general, and I was in it, as the Dude would say, with both feet and a crutch. We got some tangled, but things came my way pretty soon, and when the bears were laid out I stopped to listen. The fight was still going on down the canyon. The boy is still holding his own, I thought; it would be a pity to spoil such a battle. So I went on and dressed my bears, while the steady roll of musketry thundered in the gulch. Then I had a wash in the creek, had a smoke and sat down at the foot of a tree and fell asleep. The last I heard was a monotonous uproar indicating that the forces down the gulch were stubbornly holding their ground.

"I never did know how long I slept, but when I awoke all was quiet. Perhaps it was the silence following the cessation of hostilities that awakened me. I set out to find Boston, and groped my way down the gulch through a cloud of smoke. Presently I came to the scene of the fray. Where my hero had made his first and last stand was a stack of empty shells and the pump-gun so hot that it had set the dry leaves afire, but the bear hunter was gone. I yelled, but got no answer. I looked for tracks up and down the canyon, but there were no tracks. The kid had vanished.

"Then I climbed up the side of the canyon, high enough to see the tops of trees that stood in the bottom of the gulch. Near the scene of hostilities was a giant sugar pine, the top of which had been broken off. Boston had shinned up that tree when his ammunition gave out, and when I discovered him he was balancing himself upon the broken shaft and reaching out over his head into space for more limbs."

## CHAPTER X: YOSEMITE.

"Yosemite" is an Indian word, signifying "place of the Grizzly bear," and appropriately the Yosemite National Park is made a sanctuary for the California Grizzly by the regulations forbidding hunting or the carrying of firearms within its borders. Danger of extinction of the species, which was an imminent menace when the park was established, was averted by that act, and doubtless the bears have increased in numbers under protection of the United States. They were quite plentiful in that part of the Sierra Nevada in the early 90's, when, as State Forester, I co-operated with the first superintendent of the National Park, Capt. Wood, Fourth U. S. Cavalry, in driving out the sheep-men with their devastating flocks of "hoofed locusts," and protecting the Sierra forests from fire.

During the first two or three years of the Park's legal existence the hunting of deer was prohibited, but bear-hunting was permitted, and Captain Wood, Lieut. Davis and I devoted considerable time to the sport in the autumn of 1891. The Captain and I learned to appreciate the distinction between bear-hunting and bear-killing very keenly during that season. For example, I cut the trails of no less than thirteen bears in two days in the mountains north of Yosemite Valley and followed some of them, but although I succeeded in getting close enough to hustle two of the wanderers out of a leisurely walk into a lope, I never saw hair through my rifle sight. Having no dogs, of course, it was all still-hunting and trailing, with the long-odds chance of jumping a bear in the brush by sheer accident.

Late in the tourist season, bears came down out of the high mountains into the Yosemite Valley and made tracks in the Bridal Veil Meadows and along the stage roads, which were pointed out to visitors for their entertainment. The valley butcher reported bear sign at the place where he slaughtered beef for the hotel, and I tried roosting for bear in hope that it might prove better than still-hunting. There was a platform in a tree at the slaughtering place and I sat there through one chilly night without hearing or seeing any bear sign. The next night an eager tourist persuaded me to give him a share of the perch, and we roosted silently and patiently until after midnight. Hearing a bear coming through the brush, I touched my companion gently to attract his attention. He had fallen into a doze, and, awakening with a start at my touch he dropped his shotgun from the platform. The stock was broken, one of the hammers struck upon a log and a load of buckshot went whistling through the leaves of our tree. Then we went home. It was an accident; the man meant well, and he was very sorry, and I held my tongue.

The next afternoon I was one of a small party on a drive over the roads at the lower end of the valley, and of course had no gun, A bear broke out of the brush, crossed the road fifty yards ahead of the team, and went down to the meadow. It was not expedient to say all that occurred to me before comparative strangers; so I jumped from the buckboard, picked up a cudgel and lit out after that bear on a lope. He had a good start and when he discovered that he was being followed he clawed dirt to increase his lead and beat me out to the bank of the Merced. For a moment he hesitated about going into the swift water, but he decided that he would rather swim than listen to offensive personalities, and over the bank he plunged.

It was a relief to sit there, watching him swim the rapids, and feel free to say all the things I hadn't said to the man who dropped the gun, with a few general observations on the perversity of bears and bear-hunters' luck thrown in for good measure.

Bears were all over the place that year. They blundered into the roads at night and scared teams, broke into the cabin in Mariposa Grove and ate up all the grub and a sack of sugar pine seed worth a dollar a pound, and Captain Wood and I never got a shot in three weeks' of diligent hunting. The only man who had any luck was Lieutenant Davis; that is, not counting Private McNamara, who had bigger luck than a man who wounds a big Grizzly and runs really has coming to him. McNamara's luck will be seen later.

Davis killed two bears on the Perigord Meadows and one on Rush Creek, and wounded a large Grizzly in Devil's Gulch. It was a lucky shot that he made in the dark on Rush Creek. A troop horse had died about a quarter of a mile below the cavalry camp, on the edge of the National Park, and the men had seen bear tracks around the carcass. Davis and an Illinois preacher, who was roughing it for his health with the troopers, took their blankets one night and camped about thirty yards from the dead horse to await the coming of the bear. The moon was not due to rise until about midnight, and Davis pulled off his boots, rolled up in his blanket and went to sleep. The preacher was not sleepy, and was not entirely confident that it was bear nature to wait for moonlight before starting out on the prowl. So he made a small fire and sat beside it, toasting his toes and thinking of things.

Just before midnight Davis awoke, looked at his watch, and said: "Well, parson, it is about time for the moon to show up, and the bear is likely to come pretty soon. You'd better put out your fire."

The preacher shoved some dirt over the embers with his foot, and Davis had just returned his watch to his pocket, when the sound of the crunching of gravel was heard from the bank just above the carcass. Davis looked up and could just make out a huge dark form on the edge of the bank. He raised his carbine and fired point blank at the dark mass, and the report was answered by an angry growl. The bear leaped down the bank toward the hunters, and Davis sprang to his feet, dropping the carbine, and jumped into the creek, revolver in hand, to get into clear fighting ground. In doing so, he had to jump toward the bear, but he preferred close quarters in the creek bed, where the water was knee deep, to a scrimmage in the brush.

The preacher ran for his carbine, which was leaning against a tree twenty feet distant, but he had no opportunity to use it, for the bear made but one more plunge and fell into the water with the death gurgle in his throat. When Davis was certain that the bear was done for, he and the preacher ventured to examine the beast. They found that Davis had made one of the luckiest shots on record, having sent a carbine bullet through the heart of the big cinnamon bear, although he had taken no aim, and, when he fired, could not distinguish the bear's head from his tail.

They pulled the dead bear out of the water, and by the light of the moon, which had risen over the mountain, the preacher curiously examined the teeth and formidable claws of the first wild bear he had ever seen. He felt of the animal's enormous, muscular legs, and was profoundly impressed with the great strength of the brute.

"Well," said Davis, after he had inspected the body sufficiently, "we might as well turn in and sleep the rest of the night. The trail back to camp is too rough to follow in the night." And so saying he rolled up in his blankets.

"Sleep!" said the preacher; "sleep with those dum things wandering about! Not much." And the preacher rebuilt his fire, climbed upon a log, and roosted there, with cocked carbine, until daybreak, while the Lieutenant slept and snored.

The "other story" is about Private McNamara, a Grizzly, and some gray squirrels. McNamara got leave to go hunting, and went over to Devil's Gulch, the roughest canyon in the country and the best hiding place for big game. McNamara had good luck, and killed about a dozen gray squirrels, which he slung to his belt. He had turned homeward, and was picking his way through the fallen timber, when a Grizzly arose from behind a log about fifty yards away. McNamara raised his carbine and fired. The bear howled and started for him, and McNamara felt in his belt for another cartridge, but none was there. He had fired his last shot.

McNamara realized that he had to trust to his legs to get him out of that scrape, and he turned and ran faster than he ever sprinted in his life. But the bear was the better runner, and gained rapidly. The dangling squirrels impeded McNamara's action, and as he ran he tried to get rid of them. He pulled two loose and dropped them, and the Grizzly stopped to investigate. Bruin found them good, and he ate them in two gulps and resumed the chase.

McNamara dropped some more squirrels and gained a good lead, and then he unhooked his belt and dropped all that were left, and when the Grizzly finished the lot McNamara was out of sight across the river and getting his second wind for a long run home.

## CHAPTER XI: THE RIGHT OF WAY.

"It was pretty late in the season," said my friend, the prospector, "when I took a notion that I'd like to see what sort of a country lies north of the Umpqua River, in Oregon, and I struck into the mountains from Drain Station with my prospecting outfit and as much grub as I could pack upon my horse. After leaving Elk Creek I followed a hunting trail for a day, but after that it was rough scrambling up and down mountain sides and through gulches, and the horse and I had a pretty tough time. The Umpqua Mountains are terribly steep and wild and it's no fool of a job to cross them.

"There is any amount of game in those mountains, and where I went it never is hunted, and, therefore, not hard to find. If I had cared to shoot much, I could have killed a great many bears, but I wasn't in there for fun so much as for business, and I didn't shoot but one. Bear meat is no good at any time unless a man is starving, according to my notions, and in the summer it is worse than no good. Before berries are ripe a bear goes around clawing the bark from logs and dead trees and feeds on the borers and ants. He has a banquet when he strikes a well-populated ant heap, and then he smells and tastes like ants if you try to eat him. His meat is rank, and if you eat it for a day or two you will break out all over with a sort of rash that is mightily uncomfortable. There is no fur on a bear in summer and his skin is not worth taking, so you see there was no reason why I should fool away time and cartridges on Bruin. Besides, I rather like Bruin for his comical ways, and when he doesn't bother me, I'd rather watch him than shoot at him.

"I had to kill one big brown fellow, because he wouldn't get out of my way and my horse was afraid to pass him. He was on a narrow ridge that I was following in order to keep out of the heavy timber, and the bear sat upon his haunches right in my way. Probably he never saw a man before, for he didn't seem to be in the least disturbed when I hove in sight leading the horse. I supposed he would drop on all fours and scuttle away, but not a bit of it. He had struck something new and was going to see the whole show. There he sat, with his forepaws hanging down and his head cocked on one side, looking at the procession with the liveliest curiosity in his face. There was nothing wicked in his appearance, and if it hadn't been for the horse I think I would have passed within three yards of him without any trouble. As it was, I dragged the horse up to within twenty feet, but then he hung back, snorted and protested so vigorously that I was afraid he would back over the edge and fall down the steep mountain side.

"Letting the horse back away a few yards, I tied his halter to a scrub tree and then advanced toward the bear with my rifle in my left hand. He didn't budge, and when I yelled at him he only started a little and cocked his head over on the other side. That made me laugh, and then I amused myself by talking to him. 'Why don't you move?' said I. 'I know you got here first and have a squatter claim on the quarter-section, but you ought not to sit down on public travel in that way.' He looked at me as though I was the oddest specimen he ever came across, and scratched his ear with his left paw.

"'You musn't mind my friend here,' I said, pointing to the horse; 'he's a little shy in society, but he means well. If you'll move to one side, we'll pass on.' It was a fool sort of an idea, standing there and talking to a bear, but I was interested in studying the expression of his face and seeing how puzzled he seemed to be at the sound of my voice. He'd rub his ear or his nose once in a while, and then look up, as though he were saying: 'Just repeat that; I don't quite make out what you are driving at,' and then he'd assume a look of the most intense interest. I don't know how long he would have remained there, but I got tired of the fun and threw a stick at him. It would have hit him on the nose, but he warded it off very cleverly, and then his manner changed. He growled a little and began swaying his head from side to side, and when I saw the green glint come into his eyes--the danger signal that all the carnivorae flash and all hunters heed--I knew the time was up for airy persiflage and that I was in for a 'scambling and unquiet time' unless I promptly took up the quarrel. It was an easy shot, through the throat to the base of the skull, and the bullet smashed the spinal cord.

"That was the only bear, other than a Grizzly, that I ever saw dispute the right of way of a man through the woods."

# CHAPTER XII: WELL HEELED.

"Curious how some men will lose their grip on the truth when they talk about bears," said Mr. Jack Waddell, of Ventura. "There's old Ari Hopper, for example, a man whose word is good in a hoss trade, but when he tells about his bear fights he puts your confidence in him to an awful strain. I don't say that Ari would tell lies, but he puts a whole lot of fancy frills on his stories and fixes 'em up gorgeous. I reckon I've run across most as many bears as anybody, but I never had no such adventures as I read about.

"The most curious bear scrape I ever had was over on the Piru last spring, and just the plain facts of the case beat anything you ever heard. There was an old white-headed Grizzly in that part of the country that did a heap of damage, but nobody had been able to do him up. They set spring guns for him on the mountain and put out poison all around, but he'd beat the game every time. Taylor, of the Mutaw ranch, fixed a spring gun that he thought would fix the old fellow for sure. It was a big muzzle-loading musket, with a bore as big as an eight-gauge shotgun, and Taylor loaded it with a double handful of powder, thirty buckshot and a wagon bolt six inches long. It was set right in the trail and baited with a chunk of pork tied to the muzzle and connected with the trigger by a string.

"The gun was about a mile from the house, and the very first night after it was set, Taylor was awakened by a roar that made the windows rattle and seemed to shake the very hills. Taylor knew the old gun had gone off, and he chuckled as he thought of the wreck it made of the old Grizzly. In the morning he started out to take a look at his dead bear, and found his tracks leading from the meadow right up the trail. He knew the sign, because the Grizzly put only the heel of his off forefoot to the ground and there was a round mark in the track that looked as though it were made by the end of a bone.

"As I was saying, Taylor recognized the tracks and was sure he had got old Whitehead, but he was sort of puzzled when he noticed a hog's track in the same trail and saw that those were sometimes wiped out by the bear's tracks. When he got near the spring gun he saw bits of meat hanging in the brush, but no fur anywhere. He kept on, and pretty soon he saw a dark mass lying on the ground in front of the wreck of the old musket. He stepped up to look at it and saw that it was the mangled corpse of the biggest hog on the ranch. One of the hams was gone, and apparently it had been cut away with a knife. The head and all the fore part of the hog had been blown to flinders, and the brush was just festooned with pork.

"Taylor thought somebody had happened along and cut a ham out of the dead hog, but there were no man tracks anywhere; nothing but hog and bear tracks. It was plain that the cunning old bear had driven the hog ahead of him up the trail to spring the gun, but that missing ham could not be accounted for.

"Another curious thing was noticed about all the cattle that the Grizzly killed. Ordinarily, you know, the Grizzly strikes a blow that breaks a steer's neck or shoulder, and then pulls him down and finishes him. In the Piru country a great many cattle were found with their throats neatly cut, and old Whitehead's tracks were invariably found near the carcasses. The only man that the Grizzly ever killed, so far as is known, was a Mexican sheepherder, and he was found with a slash in the side of the head that looked like the work of a hatchet or other sharp tool. Some people didn't believe that the Mexican was killed by a bear, but there were no other tracks where his body was found, and I know for a fact that old Whitehead did kill him.

"I was pirooting around in the brush on a hill pretty well up toward the head of Piru Creek one afternoon, when I caught sight of a bear about twenty yards ahead of me. I could see only a part of his fur, and couldn't tell how he was lying or what part of him was in sight. I figured around a few minutes, but couldn't get a better sight, and so I just took chances and let drive for luck at what I could see. It was a fool thing to do, of course, but I just happened to feel careless and confident. There was a snort and a crash, and old Whitehead loomed up madder than a hornet. I had shot him in the haunch and he felt insulted. He made a rush at me, and I skipped aside and jumped for a small tree standing on the brink of a little ravine. My rifle dropped into the ravine, and I went up the tree like a monkey up a pole, and by the time the old bear had put his helm down and swung around to take a whack at me I was out of his reach and felt safe.

"The bear sat down and deliberately sized up the situation, and then he walked up to the tree and began striking at the trunk with his right paw. That made me laugh at first, but I was just paralyzed with amazement when I saw clean-cut chips flying at every stroke and caught a metallic gleam as his paw swung in the air. I didn't have much time to investigate the matter because the old Grizzly was a boss chopper and my tree began to totter very soon. I had sense enough to see that if I came down with the tree on the upper side the bear would nail me with one jump, and I threw my weight on the other side so as to fall the tree into the ravine. I thought I might have the luck to land without breaking any bones, and then I'd have quite a start of the bear and perhaps be able to pick up my rifle.

"As the tree toppled over the edge of the ravine and began to fall I swung around to the upper side and braced myself for the crash. During the fall I managed to throw my legs out over a branch, and when the tree struck bottom I shot out feet foremost, sliding down through the brushy top and landing with a pretty solid jar right side up and no damage except a few bruises and scratches. The first thing I looked for was my rifle, and, luckily, it wasn't two yards away. I grabbed it and ran up the other side of the ravine to a rocky ledge, while the Grizzly was crashing down through the brush on his side, expecting to find me under the fallen tree. Before he knew what had happened I was shooting him full of holes and he was dead in a minute.

"When I examined the dead Grizzly I found the most singular thing I ever came across. In the sole of his right forepaw was an ivory-handled bowie-knife, firmly imbedded and partly surrounded by calloused gristle as hard as bone. The handle was out of sight, but the butt of it made a knob in the heel of the bear's foot and left a mark on the ground. Evidently he walked on that heel to keep the blade from striking stones and getting dulled. That knife accounted for all the mysteries about the white-headed Grizzly.

"What's that? Mystery about how the knife got into his foot? Not at all; that's simple enough. He swallowed the knife during some fight or other, and it worked around in his system and down into his foot just as a needle does in a man."

## CHAPTER XIII: SMOKED OUT.

What a bear may do under given circumstances may be guessed with reasonable certainty by one who has had experience, but it is not always safe to risk much on the accuracy of the guess. Bruin's general nature is not to be depended upon in special cases. He has individual characteristics and eccentricities and is subject to freaks, and these variations from the line of conduct which he is expected to follow are what makes most of the trouble for people who are after his pelt. Morgan Clark, the old bear hunter of Siskiyou, never hesitates about going into a den in the winter to drive out a bear, provided the cavern is wide enough to let the bear pass him. He takes a torch in his hand and stalks boldly in, because his experience has made the proceeding seem perfectly safe.

"All you've got to do," says Morgan, "is to stand to one side and keep quiet, and the bear'll just scoot by without noticing you. It's the light that's bothering him, and all he's thinking about is getting out of that hole as fast as he can. He don't like the smoke and the fire, and he won't pay any attention to anything else until he gets outside, but then you want to look out. He goes for the first live thing in sight when he's clear of the cave and the smudge, and he don't go very slow either. Jim Brackett found that out over in Squaw Valley one day. He found a bear in a den, and built a fire at the mouth to smoke him out. The fire was burning rather slowly, Brackett thought, and he stood looking around and waiting for something to happen. While he had his back turned to the den something did happen, and it happened dog-gone sudden. That fire was plenty fast enough for the bear, and the old cuss came out without waiting to be choked. He came out galleycahoo, and the first thing he saw was Brackett leaning on his gun and waiting for the show to begin. He just grabbed Brackett by the back of the neck and slammed him around through the manzanita brush like a dog shaking a groundhog, Brackett told me that he never felt so surprised and hurt in his life. He hadn't cal'lated on that bear coming out for a good two minutes more; but mebbe the bear had stronger objections to smoking than Brackett knew. If it hadn't been for Brackett's little cur dog, that he supposed wasn't fit for nothing but barking at chipmunks, I reckon the bear would have chawed and thumped the life out of him. The cur seemed to tumble to the situation right away, and he went for the bear's heels in good shape. It generally takes time and a few knock-out cuffs from bear's paw to teach a dog that there's two ends to a bear and only one of them safe to tackle, but that little ornery kiyi knew it from the start. If there's anything a bear can't stand, it's a dog nipping his heels, and when the cur began snapping at his hind legs and yelping, he lost interest in Brackett and attended to the disturbance in the rear. The little cuss was cute and spry enough to keep out of his reach, though, and he made such a nuisance of himself, without doing any serious damage of course, that the bear got disgusted with the whole performance and hiked out through the brush. Brackett was hurt too badly to follow him or to fire a gun, and it was two months before he was able to get around. But he wouldn't have sold that little scrub cur for all the money he ever saw."

Budd Watson, who used to hunt and trap on the Pitt River and the McCloud, had an adventure with a bear that didn't conduct his part of the hunt according to Hoyle. Budd and Joe Mills tracked a big Cinnamon to a den in the mountains near the McCloud and built a big smudge to smoke him out. The wind blew the wrong way to drive the smoke in, and so Budd took a torch and went after the bear, leaving Mills on guard outside. Like Morgan Clark, he knew the bear would pass him head down and make for the open air without delay, and he wasn't afraid. When the bear got up with a growl at the appearance of the torch and started for the exit, Budd quietly stepped aside and gave him room to pass, but the Cinnamon developed individuality in an unexpected direction and made a grab for Budd's right leg as he passed. Budd threw his leg up to avoid the grab, lost his balance and fell flat on top of the bear. Instinctively he caught hold of the thick fur on the bear's hind quarters with both hands, still holding the torch in his right, but dropping his gun, and winding his legs about the bear's body he rode out into the daylight before he hardly knew what had happened.

Mills was ready to shoot when the bear appeared, but seeing his partner riding the game, he was too much surprised to take the brief chance offered at the bear's head, and in another instant it was too late. To fire after the pair had passed was too dangerous, as he might hit the rider instead of the steed. The Cinnamon, in his first panic, plunged wildly down the hill, trying to shake off his strange burden, and went so rapidly that Budd was afraid to let go. But Budd's principal fear was that the bear would recover his presence of mind and turn upon him, and his game was to keep the beast on the jump as long as he could, trusting to chance for a way out of the scrape.

The torch, made of rags soaked in oil, was still blazing in his right hand. Taking a firmer grip with his legs and a good hold just above the tail with his teeth, he applied the torch to the bear's rump. This application and the hair-raising yells of Mills, who was plunging along madly in the wake, caused an astonishing burst of speed, and the Cinnamon thundered through the brush like a runaway locomotive on a down grade, with such lurches and rolls and plunges that Budd dropped his torch and hung on, tooth and nail, for dear life.

The unfeeling Mills was taking a frivolous view of the case by this time, and as he strode rapidly along behind, losing ground at every jump, however, he encouraged Budd and the bear alternately with flippant remarks: "Stick to him, Budd! Whoaouw! Go it bar!" "You're the boss bar-buster, old man. Can't buck you off!" "Whoopee Hellitylarrup!" "Who's bossing that job, Budd; you or the bar?" "Say Budd, goin' ter leave me here? Give a feller a ride, won't ye?" "Hi-yi; that's a bully saddle bar!"

But Budd was waiting for a chance to dismount, and as the bear rose to leap a big log in his path, Budd let go all holds and slid head first to the ground. He bumped his forehead and skinned his nose on a rock. His legs and back were scratched and torn by the brush, his clothes were in tatters, and he was almost seasick from the lurching motion of his steed.

Mills came up roaring with laughter. He thought it was the funniest thing he ever had seen in his life. But Budd was not a man of much humor and he failed to appreciate the ridiculous features of the adventure. He got up slowly, ruefully brushed away the blood and dirt from his face, and solemnly and methodically gave Joe Mills the most serious and matter-of-fact licking that a man ever got in this world.

**CHAPTER XIV: A CRY IN THE NIGHT.**

In the flickering of the camp-fire the glooming wall of firs advanced and receded like the sea upon the shore, whispering, too, like the sea, of mysteries within its depths; for this is true: the wind in the forest and the wave upon the beach make the same music and tell the same strange tales. Through a rift in the darkening wall the last afterglow on the snow-cap of Mount Hood made a rosy point against the western sky, a "goodnight" flashed from the setting sun to the man by the camp-fire.

Out from the enfolding night that fell as a mantle when the light died on Mount Hood, came a shape, followed by a shadow that seemed to be with but not of the shape. Like a menacing enemy the shadow dogged the steps of the man who came out of the night, now towering over him in monstrous height against a tree trunk, now suddenly falling backward and darting swiftly down a forest aisle in panic fear, only to spring forth with gigantic leaps and grotesque waxings and wanings and inane caperings at his heels as the firelight rose and fell.

A cheery "Howdy, stranger!" drew the attention of the man by the fire--known to his Indian guide by the generic name of "Boston," which is Chinook for white man--and he returned the greeting to the tall, gray-bearded man who strode toward him, glad to have company in the absence of the Indian, Doctor Tom, who had gone down to the Columbia for supplies. A haunch of venison confirmed the stranger's brief explanation that he was hunting and made his arrival doubly welcome.

When the pipes were lighted, Boston drew the old fellow out, found that he hunted for a living and soon had a hunt for the next day all arranged. They were telling camp-fire yarns, and the stranger was speaking in an animated way of some adventure, when Boston noticed a sudden change in his expression and an abrupt halt in his speech.

Turning in the direction toward which the stranger's apprehensive gaze was directed, Boston saw a dark figure standing motionless in the shadow of a fir, and he laid his hand upon his rifle. The figure advanced into the firelight and Boston recognized Doctor Tom. The Indian said nothing, but placed his pack upon the ground in silence, and Boston saw him cast one swift, glowering look at the stranger, who was apparently trying to conceal his uneasiness under an assumption of indifference.

Doctor Tom had travelled all day and must have been hungry, but he did not take any food out of the pack or even go to the fire for a cup of tea, and he shook his head when Boston offered him a piece of broiled venison. Not a bite would he touch, but sat, silent and motionless as a statue, upon a log away from the fire and with his back turned to the stranger.

Boston tried to resume the camp-fire stories, but the grizzled hunter was thinking of something else and replied with monosyllables. Soon he arose, made up his pack, threw his rolled blanket over his shoulder and picked up his rifle. Boston, in some surprise, urged him to remain, and reminded him of the arrangement for the next day's hunt. There was a slight movement of Doctor Tom's head, and he seemed about to arise, but the almost imperceptible tension of his limbs instantly relaxed, and he remained apparently indifferent and unheeding.

"Fact is," said the stranger, "I forgot that I'd got to be up to Hood River to-morrow, and I reckon I'll just mosey along to-night so as to make it. I know the trail with my eyes shut." He was about to stride out of camp, when his eye caught Doctor Tom's old musket leaning against the tree. "You don't shoot with this?" he asked with a little, uneasy laugh, as he picked up the ancient piece and toyed with the lock. Boston laughingly replied, "Well, hardly," and the stranger replaced the gun, said "So long," and was lost in the gloom.

It was ten minutes before Doctor Tom moved, and then he got his musket and brought it to the fire. He lifted the hammer, removed the cap, and taking a pin from his waist band worked at the nipple until he extracted a splinter of wood. Then he drew the charge, blew down the barrel to see that it was clear and reloaded the musket. Doctor Tom took some smoked salmon from his pouch, made a cup of coffee and silently ate his supper, and Boston began to comprehend that there was a reason for his refusal to eat while the stranger was in camp. But it was useless to try to make Doctor Tom talk until he had smoked, and Boston waited patiently.

At last Doctor Tom said, abruptly, "You know um?" Boston replied that he did not know the stranger, told briefly how he came into camp, and by adroit questioning drew, in laconic sentences, a story from the taciturn Indian.

The man was a hunter, who had been a famous bear-killer many years ago. In the days of muzzle-loaders he had two rifles, one of which was always carried for him by an Indian whom he hired for that service. If his first shot failed to kill, he handed the empty rifle to the Indian to exchange for the second weapon, and usually brought down his bear while the Indian was reloading. A member of Doctor Tom's tribe, probably a relative, was gun-bearer for the hunter on one of his expeditions. They ran across a she-bear with cubs and the hunter shot her, but the wound only stung her, and she rushed fiercely upon him. The second shot did not stop her, and the hunter and the Indian had to turn and run for their lives.

But a Grizzly in a rage can outrun any man in a long race, and the angry she-bear rapidly overhauled her foes. The white man and the Indian ran side by side, although the Indian could have outstripped him. The red man had his knife in hand ready for the moment when the bear should seize one of them. The white man glanced over his shoulder, saw the bear lurching along within one jump of them, seized the Indian by the shoulders and hurled him backward into the very jaws of the furious brute. The white man escaped with his life, and the Indian lived just long enough to tell those who found him, a torn and bloody mass of flesh and broken bones, how he had been sacrificed to a coward's love of life.

Doctor Tom told this in his uncouth jargon of English and Chinook, without a tremor, but his black eyes glowed with a gleam of light not reflected from the dying embers of the campfire, and Boston was glad that the stranger had gone. Then he knew why Doctor Tom sat silently apart and would taste no food while the stranger was in camp. The stranger might accept Boston's hospitality and eat salt with him, but the Indian would not acknowledge by any act that he, Doctor Tom, had any interest in that camp, or bind himself by Indian custom to treat the stranger as his guest.

Boston awoke in the still dark hours before dawn and lay thinking over Doctor Tom's story and the demeanor of the man who had wandered into camp. A cry clove through the silence of the night like a lightning flash through a black cloud, and as the gloom becomes deeper after the flash, so the silence seemed more intense and oppressive after that cry. It came from across the canyon, clear and far, a cry of mortal terror.

It is a panther, thought Boston, and he listened for its repetition or an answer from the mate, but the stillness was unbroken. He turned over to see if Doctor Tom had heard or noticed it, and thought the dark bundle by the side of the log seemed rather small for the sleeping Indian. Boston got up and walked over to the log. Doctor Tom's blanket only was there. Boston looked for the musket; it was in its old place against the tree. His own rifle was undisturbed.

Boston concluded that Doctor Tom had gone for water or was off on some incomprehensible Indian freak, the reason of which was not worth a white man's time to puzzle out, rolled up in his blanket again and became oblivious to the realities around him.

It was daylight when Boston awoke again. Doctor Tom had not returned. Boston made a fire, and while cooking breakfast he noticed that the Indian's long knife was gone from the log where he had left it sticking after supper. He halloed to Tom, but received no answer save the echo. Calmly confident of Doctor Tom's ability to look out for himself, Boston went about his business without more ado, ate his breakfast and was taking a second cup of coffee when Doctor Tom came into camp, silent and grave as usual, but rather paler. He came from the direction of the canyon.

The Indian drank some coffee and then carefully took his left arm with his right hand from the bosom of his shirt, where it had been resting, and said, "Broke um." Boston examined the arm and found that it was badly bruised and broken above the elbow. He heated some water and bathed the arm and then told Tom to brace his breast against a tree and hold on with his right arm. Boston took hold of the left arm on the opposite side of the tree, braced his feet and pulled. Rough splints were soon made and applied, and a big horn of whiskey made Doctor Tom feel more comfortable. While making the splints Boston asked Tom for his knife, having carefully mislaid his own. "Lose um," said Doctor Tom, but he offered no more explanation. When asked how he broke his arm, he replied, "Fall down." Evidently he had fallen down, but there were five odd-looking marks on his throat, and Boston thought of that cry in the night and wondered if the whispering firs could tell of another mystery hidden in the forest; of a menacing shadow dogging the footsteps of a man and grappling with him in the dark.

Boston and Doctor Tom broke camp and started back over the

mountain on the Hood River trail. Boston was in the lead, and as he walked along he looked closely for the tracks of the stranger's boots, as he had said he was going to Hood River. There were no tracks. The stranger had not gone over that trail.

## CHAPTER XV: A CAMPFIRE SYMPOSIUM.

"Speaking of bears, Joe," said one of a party of hunters sitting around a campfire at old Fort Tejon, "Old Ari Hopper has had more queer experiences with bears than anybody. He has given up hunting now, but he used to be the greatest bear-killer in the mountains. Ari has a voice like a steam, fog-horn--the effects of drinking a bottle of lye one night by mistake for something else, and when he speaks in an ordinary tone you can hear him several blocks away. You can always tell when Ari comes to town as soon as he strikes the blacksmith's shop up at the cross-roads and says, 'Holloa' to the smith. Ari was out on the Alamo mountain one day and got treed by a big black bear--"

"A black bear on the Alamo?" interrupted Dad. "There ain't nothing but Grizzlies and Cinnamons over there. I was over there once--"

"Hold on, Dad, it's my turn yet. You never heard of a Grizzly climbing a tree, did you?"

"Oh, well, if you've got to have your bear go up a tree, all right. We'll call it a black bear. Besides, if it's one of Ari's bear stories, anything goes."

"The bear treed Ari," resumed the other, "and just climbed up after him in a hurry. Ari went up as high as he could and then shinned out on a long limb. The bear followed, and Art kept inching out until he got as far as he dared trust his weight. The bear was climbing out after him and the limb was bending too much for safety when Ari yelled at the bear: 'Go back, you d----d fool. You'll break this limb and kill both of us. Want to break your cussed neck, goldarn ye?'

"Well, sir, that bear stopped, looked at Ari, and then down to the ground, and then he just backed along the limb to the trunk, slid down and lit out for the brush. Ari swears that the bear understood him. Bears have a heap of sabe, but I'm inclined to think that it was Ari's stentorian roar that scared him away."

"That's one of Art's fairy tales," said Joe. "Let Ari tell it, and he has had more bear fights and killed more Grizzlies than anybody, but the fact is that his brother-in-law, Jim Freer, did all the killing. You never heard of Ari going bear hunting without Jim. When they'd find any bears Ari would go up a tree and Jim would stand his ground and do up the bear. Jim never gets excited in a scrimmage, and he's a dead shot. He'll stand in his tracks and wait for a bear, and when the brute gets near him he'll raise his rifle as steadily as though he were at a turkey shoot and put the bullet in the exact spot every time. If that had been the piebald Grizzly of the Piru that treed Art, he wouldn't have scared him out of the tree."

"What's the piebald Grizzly?" inquired Dad in an incredulous tone. "I never heard of no such bear as that."

"Oh, you needn't think I'm lying. I wouldn't lie about bears."

"How about deer?"

"Well, that's different. I never knew a hunter or any chap that likes a gun and a tramp in the mountains who wouldn't lie about a deer except Jim Bowers. He doesn't lie worth a cent. Why Bowers will go out after venison, come back without a darned thing, and then tell how many deer he shot at and missed. I've known him to miss a sleeping deer at thirty yards and come into camp and tell all about it.

When I do a thing like that I come back and lie about it. I swear I haven't seen a deer all day long."

"If you told the truth," said Dad, "we'd hear nothing but deer stories--the missing kind--all night."

"That's all right, but I'm telling about bears now. This bear I speak of is a big Grizzly that some people call Old Clubfoot. Jim Freer knows him better than anybody, I reckon. Jim got caught in a mountain fire over on the Frazier one day, and he had to hunt for water pretty lively. He found a pool about five yards across down in a gully, and he jumped in there and laid down in the water. He hadn't more than got settled when the big piebald bear came tearing along ahead of the fire and plunged into the same pool. It was no time to be particular about bedfellows, and the bear lay right down alongside of Jim in the water. They laid there pretty near half an hour as sociable as old maids at a tea party, and neither one offered to touch the other. The bear kept one eye on Jim and Jim kept both eyes on the bear, and as soon as the fire had passed Jim crawled out and scooted for camp, leaving the Grizzly in soak."

"Did you ever see that piebald Pinto of the Piru?" inquired Dad.

"Did I ever see him? Well, I had the d---dest time with him I ever had in my life except the day I was chased by a spotted mountain lion on Pine Mountain. I was hunting deer over on the Mutaw when I saw Old Clubfoot in the brush and fired at him. He turned and rushed towards me and I had just time enough to get up a tree. The tree was a pinon about a foot thick and would have been a safe refuge from any other bear, and I felt all right perched about twenty feet from the ground. But Old Clubfoot is different from other bears. He's a persistent, wicked old cuss, and would just as soon sit down at the foot of a tree and starve a man out as hunt sheep. He came up to the tree, looked it all over, sized it up, and then stood on his hind legs and took a good hold of the trunk with his arms. He couldn't quite reach me, and at first I thought he was going to climb up, which made me laugh, but I didn't laugh long. The old bear began to shake that tree until it rocked like a reed in a gale, and I had all I could do to hold on with arms and legs. It's a fact that he pretty nearly made me seasick. He shook the tree for about ten minutes, and when he saw that it was a little too stout and that he couldn't shake me down, he began tearing the trunk at the base with his teeth and claws. The way he made the bark and splinters fly was something surprising. He gnawed about half way through, and there was a wicked glitter in his little green eyes as he stood up to take another grip on the tree. I saw that he'd shake me down sure that time, and I got ready to take the last desperate chance for life. Looking around, I noticed a barranca, or gully, twenty feet wide about a hundred yards away, and I determined to make for that. If I could reach the bank, jump across and get to some heavy timber on the other side, I would be all right. Twenty feet is a big jump and I knew the bear couldn't make it. It was doubtful if I could, but a man will do some astonishing things when he's at the head of a procession of that sort. When the Grizzly began to shake, I took a firm hold on the big limb with my hands and swung clear of the trunk. He made that tree snap like a whip, and as it swayed over toward the barranca I threw my feet out ahead and I let go. I shot through the air like a stone out of a sling, and struck the ground nearly fifty yards from the tree. It was that fifty yards that saved me, for by the time I had picked myself up and started on a run the bear was coming hellitywhoop. I ran like a scared wolf and I think my momentum would have carried me across the barranca if the bank had been firm, but the earth caved under me as I took off for the leap, and down I went into the gully under a mass of loose earth. I reckon there was about a ton of dirt on top of me, and I was in danger of being smothered under it. I couldn't move a limb and I'd have passed in my chips right there and been reckoned among the mysterious disappearances if it hadn't been for the bear. The piebald Grizzly of the Piru saved my life."

"Did he dig you out?" asked Dad, grinning.

"That's what he did."

"And then he ate you up, I suppose?"

"No; I'm coming to that. The bear came tumbling down into the barranca on top of the dirt and he began to dig right away. He was as good as a steam paddy, and in a few moments I was able to get a breath of air. I was wondering-which would be the worse, smothering or being chewed up by a bear, when he raked the dirt off my head and I saw daylight. I shut my eyes, thinking I would play dead as a last ruse, when I heard a roar and a rush. There was a trembling of the ground, a dull, heavy shock, and I felt something warm on my face. At the same moment I heard a growl of rage and surprise from the bear and felt relieved of his weight above me. A terrific racket followed. As soon as I could free myself from the dirt, I crawled out cautiously and saw a strange thing. A big black bull, the boss of the Mutaw ranch, had charged on the Grizzly and knocked him over just in time to save me. One of his horns had gored the bear's neck, and it was the warm blood that I felt on my face. They were old enemies, each bore scars of wounds inflicted by the other, and they were having a battle royal down there in the barranca."

"Which licked?" inquired Dad, eagerly.

"I don't know. I'd had enough bear fight for one day, and I lit out for camp and left them clawing and charging and tearing up the ground. I didn't see any necessity for remaining as referee of that scrimmage. You remember, father, that I came into camp covered with blood, and that you thought I had been monkeying with a mountain lion."

"Ye-es, I recollect the circumstances, but I never heard about the bear and bull episode before. I seem to have sort of a dim notion that you were packing a deer home on your back and fell into a barranca with it and lost it in a mud slough, but perhaps I'm mistaken. You forgot to tell me the facts, I guess."

"Shouldn't wonder," said Dad; "Joe does sometimes forget to tell the facts, but he wouldn't lie about a bear."

"I haven't forgotten the facts about your bear trap in Sonoma," retorted Joe.

"I allow that little accident never lost anything by your telling. 'Taint worth telling nohow. You'd better turn in and go to sleep and not be telling durn lies about folks that's old enough to be your great-grandfather, but ain't too old yet to give ye a licking, b'gosh! Don't ye go to fergittin' that I'm a constable, and can arrest people who use language cal'lated to provoke a breach of the peace."

"Dad was a devil of a bear catcher," continued Joe, "and once he built a big trap up in Sonoma. The door weighed about three hundred pounds, and it took two men and a crowbar to lift it. Dad had fixed it so that no bear in Sonoma could raise it from the inside. It was a bully trap, and when it was all finished Dad set the trigger and went inside to tie the bait on. He forgot to prop the door, and as soon as he monkeyed with the trigger he set it off and down came the door with a bang. It worked beautifully.

"When Dad realized that he had caught himself he was sorry he had made such a solid door. He couldn't think of any way of getting out, and there wasn't nobody within five miles. Dad yelled for about an hour and then quit. After a while he heard something coming, and thinking it might be a neighbor riding along the trail, he shouted again. Peering out between' the logs he saw two bears in the moonlight making straight for the trap, and he stopped his noise. The bears came up, sniffed all around, smelt Dad and the bait and began clawing at the logs to get inside. Then Dad was sorry he hadn't built the trap stronger and used heavier logs. He tried to scare the bears by yelling, but the more he yelled, the harder they dug to get at him, and it wasn't long before he heard a mountain lion answering his shout and coming nearer every minute. The lion came down off the mountain, jumped on top of the trap and began tearing at the log's up there. He got his paw down through the trigger-hole, and Dad had to go to the other end of the trap to keep out of reach. Then the bears got the logs torn so that they could reach in between them in two or three places, and they kept Dad on the jump inside. Before morning there was another lion and three more bears at work on the Dad-trap, and they'd have got him by noon that next day if a party of hunters hadn't come along and scared them away. These are the facts, but Dad used to tell it differently.

"Dad said he pulled up one of the floor logs and began to dig with his knife and hands. He sunk a hole two or three feet deep and then run a drift under the trap to a big hollow tree that stood just behind it. While the bears were digging in, Dad was digging out. He struck the root of the tree with his tunnel and made an upraise to the inside of the trunk. He climbed up about ten feet and struck into a mass of honey and comb, and crawled through that to a hole about fifty feet from the ground, where he could look out. Just about that time the bears and the lions broke into the trap and began to fight over the bait. The growling and yelling were fearful, and the air was full of flying fur, bark and chips. While Dad was watching the fight he heard a great scratching and scrambling in the tree beneath him, and he knew that one of the bears had caught the scent of the honey and was following it through his drift and upraise. Dad crawled out through the bee hole, slid down the tree and lit out for home. When he came back with his boys and neighbors he found the trap chock full of dead bears and lions. He cut down the bee tree, killed the bear that was inside and got half a ton of fine honey. That's the way Dad tells it."

"I never told no such dogdurned lie as that since I was born," snorted Dad, "and my boys got me out with a crow-bar."

## CHAPTER XVI: BRAINY BEARS OF THE PECOS.

The people who live on the Pecos, away up in the canyon, almost in the afternoon shadow of Baldy and just this side of the Truchas Peaks, do not assert that the bears of that region are wiser than the bears of any other country on earth, for they are ready to admit that in this wide world are many things concerning which they know nothing. But they have never heard of any bears more thoughtful than the bears of the Pecos, and it is doubtful if anybody else ever has.

No man can associate with bears for any considerable length of time without having it impressed upon him that Ursus Americanus is nobody's fool. Senor Mariano Ortiz of the Upper Pecos affirms upon the faith of a descendant of the Conquistadores that this is so, and he ought to know, for he and the bears have been joint occupants of the ranch for years. There was a time when Senor Ortiz thought the Pecos country admirably adapted to the raising of hogs, but that was before he tried to raise hogs there and before he had learned to appreciate the mental capacities of bears.

Senor Ortiz went down to Pecos town and bought some hogs, drove them up the river, and turned them into his alfalfa field to fatten. They were of genuine thoroughbred razor-back variety, trained down to sprinting form, agile, self-reliant as mules, tougher than braided rawhide, and disorderly in their conduct. They broke through the fence the first night, went up into a quaking asp patch where there was nothing eatable, and had a scrap with two bears who thought Senor Ortiz had invested in edible pork. The hogs were wiry and pugnacious, and the circumstantial evidence plainly indicated that the bears had no walk-over. However, the bears managed to get one emaciated porker after a long chase, and they bit several samples out of him. They didn't devour the whole carcass, and they didn't try pork again for two months.

After a few days, the hogs ceased breaking out of the field, and settled down to the business of laying leaf lard upon their rugged frames, a line of conduct which merited and received the hearty approval of Don Mariano, and, as subsequent events proved, was joyously appreciated by the bears. Don Mariano was fearful that the bears, having discovered the prevalence of pork, would raid his field and introduce difficulties into the business of hog raising, and he watched the drove with some solicitude. But, to his surprise, he missed no pigs.

One evening, just at dusk, Don Mariano saw two bears come out of the woods just above the alfalfa field and waddle calmly down to the fence. He hid behind a tree and watched them. When they reached the fence they stood up and placed their forepaws upon the top rail. Thinking they were about to go a-porking, Don Mariano picked up a club and prepared to stampede them, but they made no move to climb the fence, and he waited to see what their game might be. With their paws upon the rail and their snouts resting lazily upon their paws, like two old farmers discussing the crop prospects, the bears inspected the pigs in clover. One of them presently lifted a hind foot and placed it upon the bottom rail, and Don Mariano was about to break forth with a yell, when he saw that the bear was only getting into a more lazily comfortable position. Then the bear cocked his head to one side and thoughtfully scratched his ear. The hogs were nosing around in the clover, and the whole drove was in full view of the bears. The hogs were still lean and athletic.

After contemplating the drove for about ten minutes, one of the bears turned about, walked two or three steps upright, came down to all fours, and, with a grunt, shambled slowly away. The other leisurely followed, and they disappeared in the woods. Now, Don Mariano didn't understand at the time, but he learned later that those bears were sizing up his hogs, and after inspection they had decided that there wasn't one in the lot fat enough to kill.

During the next month Don Mariano saw bears loafing about the edge of the woods or lolling over his fence at least a dozen times, and he couldn't at all make out what they were at, as they did not molest his hogs. One day he noticed with satisfaction that the hogs were improving and that one youngster, who had attended strictly to his feed, was actually growing fat. The bears must have caught on at about the same time, for that pig was missing the next morning.

From that time on the alfalfa field was raided nearly every night, and the fattest pig was taken every time. A five-string barb-wire fence proved to be no protection, and the bears wouldn't go near a spring gun, and so, to save the remnant of his drove Senor Ortiz set about building a stockade corral, so high that no bear could climb over it. It was slow work cutting, hauling and setting the logs, and when the corral was finished there was only an old sow left to be put into it.

The sow soon had a litter of a dozen pigs, and Don Mariano fed them and saw them grow with satisfaction and certainty that the bears would not get them. When they were about roasting size Don Mariano looked into the corral one morning and counted only eleven little pigs. The missing pig could not have got out, as there was no hole in the corral, and Don Mariano eyed the old sow with suspicion. Still he was inclined, like all good Mexican people, to explain inexplicable things by the simple formula: "It is the will of God," and with a shrug he dismissed the mystery from his mind.

But when he missed a second and a third little pig from the litter, he openly and violently accused the old sow of devouring her offspring, and talked of sending down to El Macho for the Padre. He did better than that, however, for he isolated the old sow in a board pen and gave the youngsters the run of the corral. A day or two later another pig mysteriously disappeared, and Don Mariano began to suspect his next door neighbor of reprehensible practices, and talked about sending for the constable. Upon second thought, he strung barb wire on the top of the stockade and set steel-traps cunningly outside. Then half a dozen little porkers were spirited away in rapid succession, and when Don Mariano satisfied himself that nobody on the Peco's had feasted upon roast pig since last Christmas, he concluded that the devil had a hand in the business for sure.

Now, Don Mariano had been heard frequently to say that he was not afraid of the devil, and truly he was no idle braggart, for he loaded up his gun and laid in wait for him inside the old sow's pen, grimly determined, if the devil swooped down after another pig, to take a shot at him flying. He felt sure of at least winging the satanic thief, for he had scratched a cross on every buckshot in the load.

It was a moonlight night. Don Mariano lay upon the clean straw that he had placed in the old sow's pen and waited for the hour of midnight, at which time, as is well known, churchyards yawn and devils flit about. He had apologized to the bereaved mother for entertaining unworthy suspicions of her, and they were on amicable terms. Don Mariano was almost dozing when he was startled broad awake by a familiar grunt. Peering between two of the posts of the stockade, he saw coming across the clearing, looming huge and distinct in the moonlight, two bears. They were headed straight for the corral. Don Mariano knew they could not climb the stockade, and he watched them with languid interest. But the corral was evidently their objective point, for they lumbered along right toward it.

"Now, look at those infatuated fool bears," said Don Mariano to himself. "They'll get into one of the traps and make a grand row and frighten the devil away, so that I won't get a shot. Por Dios!"

But the two fool bears did not get into a trap. Without delay they clambered up into a large tree beside which the corral was built, and made their way out along a big limb that hung over the corral. There was no hesitation in their movements; clearly, they had been there before. One of them, the lighter and more active, went well out toward the end of the limb, and the other advanced slowly until their combined weight bent the limb down over the top of the stockade, when the first swung himself off by his forepaws and dropped into the corral.

"That's a very smart trick," muttered Don Mariano. "You are in, no doubt of that, but how the devil you are going to get back is another story."

The bear seized a pig in no time, and having broken its neck and stopped its squealing with a dexterous right-hander on the ear, he shuffled back to a position under the limb and stood upright, holding the pig in his arms. Then the other and heavier bear moved out toward the end of the limb until it bent beneath his weight so that he could reach the pig as the lighter one held it up. The big bear took the pig, and the other bear seized the limb and drew it down until he got a firm hold with all four feet. Then the big bear backed away toward the trunk and the other followed, and the limb slowly sprang up to its natural level. The two bears backed down to the ground and waddled across the clearing, the big one walking upright and carrying the pig in his arms.

Don Mariano did not shoot. "The Good Father," he said, "has given brains like that only to such of his children as have souls. I would not commit murder for the value of a pig. Besides, I casually noticed that I had miraculously forgotten to put caps on the gun. Nevertheless I cut away all the limbs from the tree on the side toward the corral, and I still have the old sow and one pig."

## CHAPTER XVII: WHEN MONARCH WAS FREE.

For several years a large Grizzly roamed through the rugged mountain's in the northern part of Los Angeles county, raiding cattle ranges and bee ranches and occasionally falling afoul of a settler or prospector. He was at home on Mt. Gleason, but his forays took in Big Tejunga and extended for twenty or thirty miles along the range. Every settler knew the bear and had a name for him, and he went by as many aliases as a burglar in active practice. As his depredations ceased after the capture of Monarch in 1889, those who assert that Monarch was the wanderer of the Sierra Madre and Big Tejunga may be right, and some of the stories told about him may be true.

Jeff Martin, a cattleman, who lived in Antelope Valley, and drove his stock into the mountains in summer, had several meetings with the big bear, but never managed to get the best of him. When the Monarch didn't win, the fight was a draw. Jeff had an old buckskin horse that would follow a bear track as readily as a burro will follow a trail, and could be ridden up to within a few yards of the game. Jeff and the old buckskin met the Monarch on a trail and started a bear fight right away. The Monarch, somewhat surprised at the novel idea of a man disputing his right of way, stood upright and looked at Jeff, who raised his Winchester and began working the lever with great industry. Jeff was never known to lie extravagantly about a bear-fight, and when he told how he pumped sixteen forty-four calibre bullets smack into the Monarch's shaggy breast and never "fazed" him, nobody openly doubted Jeff's story.

He said the Monarch stood up and took the bombardment as nonchalantly as he would a fusilade from a pea-shooter, appearing to be only amazed at the cheek of the man and the buckskin horse. When Jeff's rifle was empty, he turned and spurred his horse back down the trail, followed by the bear, who kept up the chase about a mile and then disappeared in the brush. Jeff's theory was that the heavy mass of hair on the bear's breast effectually protected him from the bullets, which do not have great penetrating power when fired from a forty-four Winchester with a charge of only forty grains of powder.

About a week after that adventure the Monarch called at Martin's summer camp on Gleason Mountain to get some beef. It was about midnight when he climbed into the corral. The only beef in the corral that night was on the bones of a tough and ugly bull, and as soon as the Monarch dropped to the ground from the fence he got into trouble. The bull was spoiling for a fight, and he charged on the bear without waiting for the call of time, taking him amidships and bowling him over in the mud before the Monarch knew what was coming. Jeff was aroused by the disturbance and went over to see what was up. He saw two huge bulks charging around in the corral, banging up against the sides and making the dirt fly in all directions, and he heard the bellowing of the old bull and the hoarse growls of the bear. They were having a strenuous time all by themselves, and Jeff decided to let them fight it out in their own way without any interference. Returning to the cabin, he said to his son Jesse and an Indian who worked for him: "It's that d----d old Grizzly having a racket with the old bull, but I reckon the bull is old enough to take care of himself. We'll bar the door and let 'em go it."

So they barred the door and listened to the sounds of the battle. In less than a quarter of an hour the Monarch got a beautiful licking and concluded that he didn't want any beef for supper. The bull was tough, anyway, and he would rather make a light meal off the grub in the cabin. Jeff heard a great scratching and scrambling as the Monarch began climbing out of the corral. Then there was a roar and a rush, a heavy thud as the bull's forehead struck the Monarch's rear elevation, a growl of pain and surprise and the fall of half a ton or more of bear meat on the ground outside of the corral.

"I reckon the old bull has made that cuss lose his appetite," chuckled Jeff. "He won't come fooling around this ranch any more. I'll bet he's the sorest bear that ever wore hair."

The three men in the cabin were laughing and enjoying the triumph of the bull when "whang!" came something against the door, and they all jumped for their guns. It was the discomfited but not discouraged Monarch breaking into the cabin in search of his supper. With two or three blows of his ponderous paw the grizzly smashed the door to splinters, but as he poked his head in he met a volley from two rifles and a shotgun. He looked at Jeff reproachfully for the inhospitable reception, turned about and went away, more in sorrow than in anger.

Jeff Martin's next meeting with the Monarch was in the Big Tejunga. He and his son Jesse were hunting deer along the side of the canyon, when they saw a big bear in the brush about a hundred yards up the hill. Both fired at the same moment and one ball at least hit the bear. Uttering a roar of pain, the grizzly snapped viciously at his shoulder where the bullet struck, and as he turned his head he saw the two hunters, who then recognized the Monarch by his huge bulk and grizzled front. The Monarch came with a rush like an avalanche down the mountain side, breaking through the manzanita brush and smashing down young trees as easily as a man tramples down grass. His lowered head offered no fair mark for a bullet, and he came on with such speed that only a chance shot could have hit him anywhere. Jeff and his son Jess did not try any experiments of that kind, but dropped their rifles and shinned up a tree as fast as they could. They were none too rapid, as Jeff left a piece of one bootleg in the Monarch's possession. The Monarch was not a bear to fool away much time on a man up a tree, and as soon as he discovered that the hunters were out of reach he went away and disappeared in the brush. The two men came down, picked up their guns and decided to have another shot at the Monarch if they could find him. They knew better than to go into the brush after a bear, but they hunted cautiously about the edges for some time. They were sure that the Monarch was still in there, but they could not ascertain at what point. Jeff went around to windward of the brush patch and set fire to it, and then joined Jess on the leeward side to watch for the reappearance of the Monarch. The wind was blowing fresh up the canyon and the fire ran rapidly through the dry brush, making a thick smoke and great noise. When the Monarch came out he came rapidly and from an unexpected quarter, and the two hunters had just time enough to break for their tree again and get out of reach.

This time the Monarch did not leave them. He sat down at the foot of the tree and watched with malicious patience. The wind increased and the fire spread on all sides, and in a few minutes it became uncomfortably warm up the tree. The bear kept on the side of the tree opposite the advancing fire and waited for the men to come down. Jeff and Jess got a little protection from the heat by hugging the leeward side of the trunk, but it became evident that the tree would soon be in a blaze, and unless they jumped and ran within the next minute or two they would be surrounded by fire. They hoped that the Grizzly would weaken first, but he showed no signs of an intention to leave. When the flames began crawling up the windward side of the tree and the heat became unbearable, Jeff said:

"Jess, which would you rather take chances on, Grizzly or fire?"

"Dad, I think I'll chance the bear," replied Jess, covering his face with his arm.

"All right. When I say go, jump and run as though you were scooting through hell with a keg of powder under your arm."

Jeff and Jess crawled out on the limbs and swung by their hands for a moment, and at the word they dropped to the ground within ten feet of the bear and lit out like scared wolves. They broke right through the burning brush, getting their hair singed as they went. The bear started after them, but he was afraid to go through the fire, and while he was finding a way out of the circle of burning brush and timber, Jeff and Jess struck out down the mountain side, making about fifteen feet at a jump, and never stopped running until they got to the creek and out of the bear's sight.

## CHAPTER XVIII: HOW OLD PINTO DIED.

This is an incredible bear story, but it is true. George Gleason told it to a man who knew the bear so well that he thought the old Pinto Grizzly belonged to him and wore his brand, and as George is no bear hunter himself, but is a plain, ordinary, truthful person, there is not the slightest doubt that he related only the facts. George said some of the facts were incredible before he started in. He had never heard or read of such tenacity of life in any animal. But there are precedents, even if George never heard of them.

The vitality of the California Grizzly is astonishing, as many a man has sorrowful reason to know, and the tenacity of the Old Pinto's hold on life was remarkable, even among Grizzlies. This Pinto was a famous bear. His home was among the rocks and manzanita thickets of La Liebra Mountain, a limestone ridge southwest of Tehachepi that divides Gen. Beale's two ranches, Los Alamos y Agua Caliente and La Liebra, and his range was from Tejon Pass to San Emigdio.

His regular occupation was killing Gen. Beale's cattle, and the slopes of the hills and the cienegas around Castac Lake were strewn with the bleached bones of his prey. For twenty years that solitary old bear had been monarch of all that Gen. Beale surveyed--to paraphrase President Lincoln's remark to Surveyor-General Beale himself--and wrought such devastation on the ranch that for years there had been a standing reward for his hide.

Men who had lived in the mountains and knew the old Pinto's infirmity of temper were wary about invading his domains, and not a vaquero could be induced to go afoot among the manzanita thickets of the limestone ridge. The man who thought he owned the Pinto followed his trail for two months many years ago and learned many things about him; among others that the track of his hind foot measured fourteen inches in length and nine inches in width; that the hair on his head and shoulders was nearly white; that he could break a steer's neck with a blow of his paw; that he feared neither man nor his works; that while he would invade a camp with leisurely indifference, he would not enter the stout oak-log traps constructed for his capture; and finally, that it would be suicide to meet him on the trail with anything less efficient than a Gatling gun.

Old Juan, the vaquero, who lived in a cabin on the flat below the alkaline pool called Castac Lake, was filled with a fear of Pinto that was akin to superstition. He told how the bear had followed him home and besieged him all night in the cabin, and he would walk five miles to catch a horse to ride two miles in the hills. To him old Pinto was "mucho diablo," and a shivering terror made his eyes roll and his voice break in trembling whispers when he talked of the bear while riding along the cattle trails.

Once upon a time an ambitious sportsman of San Francisco, who wanted to kill something bigger than a duck and more ferocious than a jackrabbit, read about Pinto and persuaded himself that he was bear-hunter enough to tackle the old fellow. He went to Fort Tejon, hired a guide and made an expedition to the Castac. The guide took the hunter to Spike-buck Spring, which is at the head of a ravine under the limestone ridge, and showed to him the footprints of a big bear in the mud and along the bear trail that crosses the spring. One glance at the track of Pinto's foot was sufficient to dispel all the dime-novel day dreams of the sportsman and start a readjustment of his plan of campaign. After gazing at that foot-print, the slaying of a Grizzly by "one well-directed shot" from the "unerring rifle" was a feat that lost its beautiful simplicity and assumed heroic proportions. The man from San Francisco had intended to find the bear's trail, follow it on foot, overtake or meet the Grizzly and kill him in his tracks, after the manner of the intrepid hunters that he had read about, but he sat down on a log and debated the matter with the guide. That old-timer would not volunteer advice, but when it was asked he gave it, and he told the man from San Francisco that if he wanted to tackle a Grizzly all by his lonely self, his best plan would be to stake out a calf, climb a tree and wait for the bear to come along in the night.

So the man built a platform in the tree, about ten feet from the ground, staked out a calf, climbed up to the platform and waited. The bear came along and killed the calf, and the man in the tree saw the lethal blow, heard the bones crack and changed his plan again. He laid himself prone upon the platform, held his breath and hoped fervently that his heart would not thump loudly enough to attract the bear's intention. The bear ate his fill of the quivering veal, and then reared on his haunches to survey the surroundings. The man from San Francisco solemnly assured the guide in the morning, when he got back to camp, that when Pinto sat up he actually looked down on that platform and could have walked over to the tree and picked him off like a ripe persimmon, and he thanked heaven devoutly that it did not come into Pinto's head that that would be a good thing to do. So the man from San Francisco broke camp and went home with some new and valuable ideas about hunting Grizzlies, chief of which was the very clear idea that he did not care for the sport.

This is the sort of bear Old Pinto was, eminently entitled to the name that Lewis and dark applied to his tribe--Ursus Ferox. Of course he was called "Old Clubfoot" and "Reelfoot" by people who did not know him, just as every big Grizzly has been called in California since the clubfooted-bear myth became part of the folk lore of the Golden State, but his feet were all sound and whole. The Clubfoot legend is another story and has nothing to do with the big bear of the Castac.

Pinto was a "bravo" and a killer, a solitary, cross-grained, crusty-tempered old outlaw of the range. What he would or might do under any circumstances could not be predicated upon the basis of what another one of his species had done under similar circumstances. The man who generalizes the conduct of the Grizzly is liable to serious error, for the Grizzly's individuality is strong and his disposition various. Because one Grizzly scuttled into the brush at the sight of a man, it does not follow that another Grizzly will behave similarly. The other Grizzly's education may have been different. One bear lives in a region infested only by small game, such as rabbits, wood-mice, ants and grubs, and when he cannot get a meal by turning over flat rocks or stripping the bark from a decaying tree, he digs roots for a living. He is not accustomed to battle and he is not a killer, and he may be timorous in the presence of man. Another Grizzly haunts the cattle or sheep ranges and is accustomed to seeing men and beasts flee before him for their lives. He lives by the strong arm, takes what he wants like a robber baron, and has sublime confidence in his own strength, courage and agility. He has killed bulls in single combat, evaded the charge of the cow whose calf he has caught, stampeded sheep and their herders. He is almost exclusively carnivorous and consequently fierce. Such a bear yields the trail to nothing that lives. That is why Old Pinto was a bad bear.

So long as Pinto remained in his dominions and confined his maraudings to the cattle ranges, he was reasonably safe from the hunters and perfectly safe from the settler and his strychnine bottle, but for some reasons of his own he changed his habits and his diet and strayed over to San Emigdio for mutton. Perhaps, as he advanced in years, the bear found it more difficult to catch cattle, and having discovered a band of sheep and found it not only easy to kill what he needed, but great fun to charge about in the band and slay right and left in pure wanton ferocity, he took up the trade of sheep butcher. For two or three years he followed the flocks in their summer grazing over the vast, spraddling mesas of Pine Mountain, and made a general nuisance of himself in the camps. There have been other bears on Pine Mountain, and the San Emigdio flocks have been harassed there regularly, but no such bold marauder as Old Pinto ever struck the range. Other bears made their forays in the night and hid in the ravines during the day, but Pinto strolled into the camps at all hours, charged the flocks when they were grazing and stampeded Haggin and Carr's merinos all over the mountains.

The herders, mostly Mexicans, Basques and Portuguese, found it heart-breaking to gather the sheep after Pinto had scattered them, and moreover they were mortally afraid of the big Grizzly and took to roosting on platforms in the trees instead of sleeping in their tents at night. Worse than all else, the bear killed their dogs. The men were instructed by the boss of the camp to let the bear alone and keep out of his way, as they were hired to herd sheep and not to fight bears, but the dogs could not be made to understand such instructions and persisted in trying to protect their woolly wards.

The owners were accustomed to losing a few hundred sheep on Pine Mountain every summer, and figured the loss in the fixed charges, but when Pinto joined the ursine band that followed the flocks for a living, the loss became serious and worried the majordomo at the home camp. So another reward was offered for the Grizzly's scalp and the herders were instructed to notify the Harris boys at San Emigdio whenever the bear raided their flocks.

Here is where Gleason's part of the story begins. The bear attacked a band of sheep one afternoon, killed four and stampeded the Mexican herder, who ran down the mountain to the camp of the Harris boys, good hunters who had been engaged by the majordomo to do up Old Pinto. Two of the Harris boys and another man went up to the scene of the raid, carrying their rifles, blankets and some boards with which to construct a platform. They selected a pine tree and built a platform across the lower limbs about twenty feet from the ground. When the platform was nearly completed, two of the men left the tree and went to where they had dropped their blankets and guns, about a hundred yards away. One picked up the blankets and the other took the three rifles and started back toward the tree, where the third man was still tinkering the platform.

The sun had set, but it was still twilight, and none of the party dreamed of seeing the bear at that time, but within forty yards of the tree sat Old Pinto, his head cocked to one side, watching the man in the tree with much evident interest. Pinto had returned to his muttons, but found the proceedings of the man up the tree so interesting that he was letting his supper wait.

The man carrying the blankets dropped them and seized a heavy express rifle that some Englishman had left in the country. The other man dropped the extra gun and swung a Winchester 45-70 to his shoulder. The express cracked first, and the hollow-pointed ball struck Pinto under the shoulder. The 45-70 bullet struck a little lower and made havoc of the bear's liver. The shock knocked the bear off his pins, but he recovered and ran into a thicket of scrub oak. The thicket was impenetrable to a man, and there was no man present who wanted to penetrate it in the wake of a wounded Grizzly.

The hunters returned to their camp, and early next morning they came back up the mountain with three experienced and judicious dogs. They had hunted bears enough to know that Pinto would be very sore and ill-tempered by that time, and being men of discretion as well as valor, they had no notion of trying to follow the dogs through the scrub oak brush. Amateur hunters might have sent the dogs into the brush and remained on the edge of the thicket to await developments, thereby involving themselves in difficulties, but these old professionals promptly shinned up tall trees when the dogs struck the trail. The dogs roused the bear in less than two minutes, and there was tumult in the scrub oak. Whenever the men in the trees caught a glimpse of the Grizzly they fired at him, and the thud of a bullet usually was followed by yells and fierce growlings, for the hear is a natural sort of a beast and always bawls when he is hurt very badly. There is no affectation about a Grizzly, and he never represses the instinctive expression of his feelings. Probably that is why Bret Harte calls him "coward of heroic size," but Bret never was very intimately acquainted with a marauding old ruffian of the range.

The hunters in the trees made body shots mostly. Twice during the imbroglio in the brush the bear sat up and exposed his head and the men fired at it, but as he kept wrangling with the dogs, they thought they missed. This is the strange part of the story, for some of the bullets passed through the bear's head and did not knock him out. One Winchester bullet entered an eye-socket and traversed the skull diagonally, passing through the forward part of the brain. A Grizzly's brain-pan is long and narrow, and a bullet entering the eye from directly in front will not touch it. Wherefore it is not good policy to shoot at the eye of a charging Grizzly. Usually it is equally futile to attempt to reach his brain with a shot between the eyes, unless the head be in such a position that the bullet will strike the skull at a right angle, for the bone protecting the brain in front is from two and a half to three inches thick, and will turn the ordinary soft bullet. One of the men did get a square shot from his perch at Pinto's forehead, and the 45-70-450 bullet smashed his skull.

The shot that ended the row struck at the "butt" of the Grizzly's ear and passed through the base of the brain, snuffing out the light of his marvelous vitality like a candle.

Then the hunters came down from their roosts, cut their way into the thicket and examined the dead giant. Counting the two shots fired the night before, one of which had nearly destroyed a lung, there were eleven bullet holes in the bear, and his skull was so shattered that the head could not be saved for mounting. Only two or three bullets bad lodged in the body, the others having passed through, making large, ragged wounds and tearing the internal organs all to pieces.

The skin, which weighed over one hundred pounds, was taken to Bakersfield, and the meat that had not been spoiled by bullets was cut up and sold to butchers and others. Estimating the total weight from the portions that were actually tested on the scales, the butchers figured that Pinto weighed 1100 pounds. The 1800 and 2000-pound bears have all been weighed by the fancy of the men who killed them, and the farther away they have been from the scales the more they have weighed.

There is no other case on record of a bear that continued fighting with a smashed skull and pulped brains, although possibly such cases may have occurred and never found their way into print. Gleason saw Old Pinto shortly after the fight and examined the head, and there is no reason to doubt his description of the effect of the bullets.

## CHAPTER XIX: THREE IN A BOAT.

The Cascade Mountains in Oregon and Washington Territory are full of bears, and as the inhabitants seldom hunt them, the animals are disposed to be sociable and neighborly and wander about close to the settlements. Harry Dumont and Rube Fields had a very sociable evening with a black bear at the Upper Cascades on the Columbia some years ago. They were crossing in a boat above the falls, when Dumont, sitting in the stern, pointed out what he said was a deer, swimming the river, about a hundred yards away. Rube bent to the oars and pulled towards the head that could just be seen on the water, intending to give Dumont a chance to knock the deer on the skull with a paddle and tow the venison ashore. When the bow of the boat ran alongside the head the supposed deer reached up, caught hold of the boat and clambered aboard without ceremony. It was a black bear of ordinary size, but it was large enough to make two men think twice before attacking it with oars. The bear quietly settled himself on the seat in the bow of the boat and looked apprehensively at the men, who were so astonished that they did not know whether to jump overboard or prepare for a fight. As the bear made no hostile movement they decided not to pick a quarrel. The boat meanwhile had drifted down stream and got into swift water, and Rube Fields saw that he must row for all he was worth to avoid going over the falls, which would be sure death. The bear seemed to realize the danger and acted as though he was uncertain whether it were better to stay aboard or take to the water again.

"Pull! pull for the shore!" urged Dumont, in a hoarse whisper, and Rube bent to the oars with all his muscle, glancing nervously over his shoulder at the silent passenger in the bow. The bear kept one eye suspiciously on the men and the other on the distant shore, and gave every indication of great perturbation of spirit. It was a hard pull to get the heavily-laden boat out of the current, but Rube finally accomplished it and rowed into safer water. He hoped that the bear would slide overboard and abandon the boat, as it made him nervous to have such a passenger behind him, and it was awkward rowing with his head turned over his shoulder all the time. He suggested to Dumont that they make a rush for the bear and pitch him out, but Dumont declined and told him to pull ashore as fast as he could. Rube pulled, and as soon as the boat's prow grated on the sand, the bear made a hasty and awkward plunge over the side, scrambled up the bank with his head cocked over his shoulder to see if there was any pursuit, and galloped away into the woods in evident fear.

Rube Fields wiped the perspiration from his brow with his forearm and fervently said, "Thank the Lord!"

Dumont gazed after the galloping bear and murmured, "Wellibedam!"

## CHAPTER XX: A PROVIDENTIAL PROSPECT HOLE.

One-eyed Zeke, who hunted for a living along Owen River, in Inyo County, Cal., in the early seventies, claimed to have a method of killing bears that might be effective if a man had nerve enough to work it and a gun that never missed fire. He carried a revolver and a heavy double-barrelled shotgun, but never a rifle, and when he saw a Grizzly he said he opened on him with the six-shooter and plugged him often enough to leave the bear in no doubt as to the source of the annoyance. Standing in plain view with the heavily-loaded shotgun ready, he awaited the charge, and at close quarters turned loose both barrels into the bear's chest.

That sounds like a plausible scheme. The heavy charges of shot at close range smash the Grizzly's interior works in a deplorable manner and he dies right away. But only a few men have the nerve to face a big ugly bear in full charge and reserve fire until he is within two yards of the muzzle of the gun. One-eyed Zeke and a celebrated hunter of the Bad Lands are the only men I have known who professed to have acquired the habit of hunting the Grizzly in such a fashion, and the celebrated Bad Lands ranchman did his killing with a rifle and always shot for the eye, which was the more remarkable because he was very near-sighted and wore eyeglasses.

Zeke once met a bear in the mountains near Owen Lake and played his customary game, but not with complete success. By some extraordinary bad luck both cartridges in his gun had defective primers, and when he pulled the triggers he was very much pained and disappointed by the absence of the usual loud report. It was a critical moment for Zeke. It took him the thousandth part of a second to grasp the situation and spring desperately to the right. Another small fraction of a second was consumed in his unexpected descent to the bottom of an old prospect hole that was overgrown with brush and had escaped his notice.

Probably that was the only prospect hole in that part of the Sierra Nevada, and it must have been dug by some half-cracked Forty-niner like Marshall, who prospected all the way from Yuma to the Columbia. Zeke vows it was dug by Providence.

The sudden and unaccountable disappearance of the man with a gun surprised the bear, and he had thrown himself forward and plunged into the chaparral several yards before he began to catch on to the fact that Zeke was not before him. As soon as Zeke struck bottom, he looked up to see if the bear was coming down too, and then he removed the bad cartridges and quickly inserted two more in his gun. He knew the bear would smell him out very soon.

In half a minute the bear's snout appeared at the top of the hole. It disappeared and was at once replaced by the bear's hind legs. Caleb was coming down stern foremost after the noxious person who had fired bullets at him. As the bear scrambled down, Zeke aimed just under his shoulder and sent two handsful of buckshot careering through his vitals in a diagonal line. The wound was almost instantly fatal, and the bear came down in a heap at the bottom of the hole, which was about ten or twelve feet deep.

The excitement being over, Zeke realized that he had been injured in the fall, and that standing up was painful. He sat down on the bear to rest and reflect, and to induce reflection he took out his pipe and lighted it. The flare of the match lighted up the prospect hole, and Zeke was interested on seeing a good-sized rattlesnake lying dead under his feet, its head crushed by his boot heel. He had landed on the snake when he fell in the hole, and the slipping of his foot sprained the ankle.

Zeke had a hard time climbing out of the prospect hole and getting back to camp, but he got there and sent some men up to hoist the bear to the surface. The Grizzly's weight was estimated to be 900 pounds, and it grew every time Zeke told the story until the last time I heard it, when it was just short of a ton.

\* \* \* \* \*

Zeke's bear-killing exploits with a scatter gun may be classed with the "important if true" information of the newspapers, but there is at least one authentic instance of the killing of a grizzly with a charge of bird shot.

Dr. H. W. Nelson, who was in later years a prominent surgeon of Sacramento, practiced medicine in Placer county, Cal., in the early fifties and was something of a sportsman. He was out quail shooting one day with a double shotgun and was making his way up a ravine in a narrow trail much choked with chaparral, when some men on the hill above him shouted to him that a wounded bear was coming down the ravine and warned him to get out of the way. The sides of the ravine were too steep to be climbed, and the noise made by the bear breaking the brush told him that it was too late to attempt to escape by running. So the doctor cocked his gun, backed into the chaparral as far as he could and hoped the bear might pass him without seeing him.

In another moment the Grizzly broke through the brush with a full head of steam directly at the doctor, and the bear's snout was within three feet of the muzzle of the gun when the doctor instinctively pulled both triggers. The two charges of small shot followed the nasal passage and caved in the front of the bear's skull, killing him instantly, but the animal's momentum carried him forward, and he and the doctor went down together. The doctor suffered no injury from the bear's teeth or claws, but was bruised by the shock of the collision and the fall.

## CHAPTER'XXI: KILLED WITH A BOWIE.

The favorite weapon of the bear hunter of the old time Wild West story book was the bowie, and doughty deeds he used to do with it in hand-to-claw encounters with monstrous Grizzlies.

It was the fashion in those days for bears to stand erect and wrestle catch-as-catch-can, trying to get the under-hold and hug the hunter to death, and the hunter invariably stepped in and plunged his bowie to the hilt in the heart of his foe. But the breed of Grizzly that hugged and the type of hunter who slew with the knife became extinct so long ago that no specimens can be found in these days.

I have known many bear slayers, but never one who would say that he ever did or would deliberately attack a Grizzly with a knife, or that he should expect to survive if forced to defend himself with such a weapon. Neither did I ever hear of a Grizzly that tried to kill a man by hugging him.

The only case of successful use of the bowie in defence against a Grizzly that seemed to be well authenticated, among all the stories I heard from hunters, was that of Jim Wilburns' fight in Trinity. Wilburn was a noted hunter and mountaineer of Long Ridge, and he had the scars to show for proof of the story. His left arm was crippled, the hand curled up like a claw, and the end of a broken bone made an ugly knob on his wrist. On his scalp were two deep scars extending from his forehead almost to the nape of his neck.

Wilburn had chased a big Grizzly into the brush and was unable to coax him out where he could get a shot at the beast. An Indian offered to go in and prospect for bear, and disappeared in the thicket. His search was successful, but perhaps it was a question whether he found the bear or the bear found him. The Indian came out of the thicket at a sprinting gait with the bear a good second, and they came so suddenly that even Jim Wilburn was taken by surprise. In two more jumps the bear would have been on top of the Indian, but Jim sprang between them, rifle in hand.

Before he could fire, the weapon was wrenched from his hands and broken like a reed. He grabbed his pistol, and that was knocked out of his hand in a jiffy. Then the bear closed on him and both went down, the bear on top. The first thing the bear did was to try to swallow Jim's head, but it was a large head and made more than a mouthful. The bear's long upper teeth slipped along the skull, ploughing great furrows in Jim's scalp, while the lower teeth lacerated his face.

Before the bear could make another grab at his head, Jim thrust his left fist down the animal's throat and kept it there while the Grizzly chewed his arm into pulp. Meanwhile he had got hold of his big knife and plunged it into the bear's side with all his strength. Again he tried to stab his enemy, but the knife did not penetrate the hide, and he discovered that in the first thrust the knife had struck a rib and the point was turned up.

The bear clawed and chawed, and Jim felt around for the wound he had made first. When he found it he thrust the knife in and worked it around in a very disquieting way. In the struggle the knife slipped out of the hole several times, and once Jim lost it, but he persistently searched for the hole when he recovered the knife and prospected for the bear's vitals.

At last he worked the blade well into the Grizzly's interior and made such havoc by turning it around that the brute gave up the fight and rolled over dead, with Jim's mangled left arm in his jaws.

It was a tough fight and a close call and old Jim was laid up in his cabin for many a day afterward.

## CHAPTER XXII: A DENFUL OF GRIZZLIES.

A man from San Gabriel Canyon came into Los Angeles and told bear stories to the Professor and the Professor told them to other people. The main point of the man's tale was that he had found a den inhabited by two Grizzlies of great size and fierce aspect. He had seen the bears and was mightily afraid of them, and he wanted somebody to go up there and exterminate them so that he might work his mining claim unmolested and unafraid. The Professor, being guileless and confiding, believed the tale, and he tried to oblige the bear-haunted miner by promoting an expedition of extermination. Seventeen men replied to his overtures with the original remark that they "Hadn't lost any bears." Since 1620 that has been the standard bear joke of the North American continent, and its immortality proves that it was the funniest thing that ever was said.

At last the Professor found a man who did not know the joke, and that man straightway consented to go to the rescue of the bear-beleaguered denizen of San Gabriel Canyon. He and three others went into the mountains with guns loaded for bear, which was an error of judgment--they should have been loaded for the tellers of bear tales. An expedition properly outfitted to hunt bear liars rather than bear lairs could load a four-horse wagon with game in the San Gabriel Canyon.

Old Bill, who had lived in the canyon many years, sorrowfully admitted that the canyon's reputation for harboring persons of unimpeachable veracity was not what it should be. The man-who-was-afraid-of-bears could not be depended upon to give bed-rock facts about bears, but he, Old Bill, was a well of truth in that line and had some good horses and burros to let to bear hunters. He, Old Bill, had killed many bears in the canyon, but had left enough to provide entertainment for other hunters. His last bear killing was heaps of fun. He ran across three in a bunch, shot one, drowned another in the creek, and jumped upon the third, and "just stomped him to death." As for the man up the creek, who pretended to have found a den of bears, he had been telling that story for so many years that he probably believed it, but nobody else did. The man up the creek had the nerve to pretend that his favorite pastime was fighting Grizzlies with a butcher knife, and anybody acquainted with bears ought to size up that sort of a man easy enough, said Old Bill.

The man up the creek, the original locator of the denful of Grizzlies, had his opinion of Old Bill as a slayer of bears. It was notorious in the canyon that the only bear Old Bill ever saw was a fifty-pound cub that stole a string of trout from under Bill's nose, waded the creek and went away while Old Bill was throwing his gun into the brush and hitching frantically along a fallen spruce under the impression that he was climbing a tree. As for himself, he was getting too old and rheumatic to hunt, but he had had a little sport with bears in his time. He recalled with especial glee a little incident of ten or a dozen years ago. He had been over on the Iron Fork hunting for a stray mule, and he was coming back through the canyon after dark. It was darker than a stack of black cats in the canyon, and when he bumped up against a bear in the trail he couldn't see to get in his favorite knife play--a slash to the left and a back-handed cut to the right, severing the tendons of both front paws--and so he made a lunge for general results, and then shinned up a sycamore tree. To his great surprise he heard the bear scrambling up the tree behind him, and he crawled around to the other side of the trunk and straddled a big branch in the fork, where he could get a firm seat and have the free use of his right arm. He could just make out the dark bulk of the bear as the beast crawled clumsily up the slanting trunk in front of him, and as the bear's left arm came around and clasped the trunk, he chopped at it with his heavy knife. The bear roared with pain. Instantly he lunged furiously at the bear's body just under the arm pit, driving the knife to the hilt two or three times, and with a moan the beast let go all holds and fell heavily to the ground.

For a minute all was silent. Then the growling began again, and he heard the scratching of claws upon the tree. In another moment the dark bulk of the bear appeared again in front of him, and again he drove the knife to the hilt into his body and felt the hot blood spurt over his hand. Clawing, scratching and yelling, the bear slid back down the tree and bumped heavily on the ground, but in a moment resumed the attack and climbed the tree as quickly as if he were fresh and unwounded.

The man up the tree was puzzled to account for such remarkable vitality and perseverance, but he braced himself for the combat, and at the proper moment chopped viciously at the bear's forearm and felt the blade sink into the bone. This time he got in three good hard lunges under the arm, and when the bear fell "ker-flop" he had no doubt that the fight was ended.

But there never was another such bear as that one. It wasn't a minute before the whole thing had to be done over again, and the man up the tree varied the performance by reaching around and giving the bear a whack in the neck that nearly cut his head off. This sort of thing was repeated at intervals for two or three hours, but at last the attacks ceased, and all was still at the foot of the tree. The man was weary, and to tell the truth a little rattled. He did not deem it wise to come off his perch and take any chance of trouble on the ground, so he strapped himself to the branch with his belt and fell asleep.

It was gray dawn when he awoke. He rubbed his eyes and looked down at the ground. Then he rubbed them again and pinched himself and glanced around at the rocks and trees to make sure that he was not in a trance. He said to himself, being a reader of the poets, "Can such things be, or is visions about?"

It was no dream and the man up the canyon said it was no lie. Lying about the foot of the sycamore were nine dead bears, weltering in their gore.

Which explains why the Don and the Colonel and the rest of the expedition of extermination returned forthwith to Los Angeles without having seen a bear. There are no more bears. The man up the canyon killed them all years ago.

THE END